THE NEW

Bussy D'Ambois

THE NEW MERMAIDS

General Editors
BRIAN MORRIS
Principal: St Davids University College, Lampeter

BRIAN GIBBONS
Professor of English Literature: University of Leeds

Bussy D'Ambois

GEORGE CHAPMAN

Edited by
MAURICE EVANS

LONDON/ERNEST BENN LIMITED

NEW YORK/W. W. NORTON AND COMPANY INC.

First published in this form 1965
by Ernest Benn Limited
25 New Street Square · Fleet Street · London · EC4A 3JA
& Sovereign Way · Tonbridge · Kent TN9 1RW

Second impression 1981
© Ernest Benn Limited 1965
Published in the United States of America by
W. W. Norton and Company Inc.
500 Fifth Avenue, New York, N.Y. 10036

Distributed in Canada by
The General Publishing Company Limited · Toronto

Printed in Great Britain

British Library Cataloguing in Publication Data

Chapman, George, 1559.–1634
    Bussy d'Ambois.
    I. Title II. Evans, Maurice
    822′.3   PR2447.B7

ISBN 0-510-33306-0
ISBN 0-393-90001-0 (U.S.A.)

CONTENTS

ACKNOWLEDGEMENTS

The following texts and works of reference have been consulted:

Bartlett, P. B., The Poems of George Chapman.
   New York, 1941.
Boas, F. S., *Bussy D'Ambois* and *The Revenge of
   Bussy D'Ambois*. 1905.
Brooke, N. S., *Bussy D'Ambois*. The Revels Plays.
   Methuen, 1964.
Jacquot, J., *Bussy D'Ambois*. Aubier, Paris, 1960.
McIlwraith, A. K., *Bussy D'Ambois. Five Stuart
   Tragedies*. World's Classics, 1953.
Nicoll, A., Chapman's Homer. Vol I. *The Iliad*.
   Vol II. *The Odyssey* and *Lesser Homerica*.
   London, 1957.
Parrott, T. M., *The Tragedies of Chapman*. 1910.
Bamborough, J. B., *The Little World of Man*.
   Longman, 1952.
Ferguson, A. S., 'The Plays of George Chapman.'
   Modern Language Review. XIII. 1918.
Schoell, F. L., *Études sur l'Humanisme continental en
   Angeleterre à la Fin de la Renaissance*.
   Paris, 1926.
Tilley, M. P., *A Dictionary of the Proverbs in
   England in the Sixteenth and Seventeenth
   centuries*. Ann Arbor, 1950.

INTRODUCTION

THE AUTHOR

GEORGE CHAPMAN was born, probably, in 1559, in Hitchin, Hertfordshire. His father was a small landowner from whom he inherited £100 and the title of 'gentleman'; but he was connected on his mother's side with the family of Grimestone who, throughout the XVIth century, were involved in government service in France—in espionage for Walsingham or liaison between Elizabeth and Henry of Navarre. He was a friend and kinsman of Edward Grimestone, the translator of French histories, on whose *General Inventorie of the Historie of France*, published in 1607, he drew for his plays about Biron; and his Grimestone connection has a bearing on his interest in contemporary French history and perhaps, too, on the early years of his career. There is a tradition that he went to Oxford but left without a degree, and it seems likely that he served in the wars of the Low Countries for all or most of the period between 1582 and 1591. There is a reference in his poems to an episode under General John Norris at Ghent in 1582, when the 'Gallick Monsieur' of *Bussy D'Ambois* was present,[1] and another to the siege of Nymeheghen in 1591[2], which suggest first-hand knowledge. He was back in England by 1594 when his earliest poem, *The Shadow of Night*, was published, and for the rest of his career seems to have been dogged by a chronic shortage of money. He was twice in gaol for debt as well as being in a number of law suits, and he was consistently unlucky in his choice of patrons. His early poems were dedicated to Raleigh or those whose names have been associated with him. His *Shadow of Night* (1594) and *Ovid's Banquet of Sense* (1595) were dedicated to Roydon, a minor poet implicated with Raleigh in the charges of blasphemy made against Marlowe; his *De Guiana* (1596) praised Raleigh's colonial aspirations; his *Hero and Leander* (1598) completed what Marlowe had left unfinished at his death, and the Epistle accom-

---

[1] *The Crowne of all Homer's Workes:* ed. Nicoll, Vol. II. Dedicatory epistle to Somerset. Ll. 84–104.

[2] *The Shadow of Night:* Hymnus in Cynthiam. Ll. 328–49.

panying *Achilles' Shield* in the same year is a moving complaint of his poverty dedicated to the mathematician, Thomas Harriot, who was a member of Raleigh's household. It has been suggested that his association with this group made him one of the targets for Shakespeare's satire on the so-called 'School of Night' in *Love's Labour's Lost*.[1] Raleigh, however, fell out of court favour and Chapman turned to the ill-fated Essex to whom he dedicated his *Seaven Bookes of the Iliades* in 1598. With the new reign Chapman gained the valuable patronage of James' eldest son, Prince Henry, to whom he dedicated *The Teares of Peace* (1609) and his complete translation of the *Iliad* in 1611. Henry, however, died in 1612, and Chapman sought the patronage of Robert, Earl of Somerset, to whom he offered his translation of the *Odyssey* in 1615. In 1616, Somerset was imprisoned and Chapman's poverty seems to have driven him from London, perhaps to the shelter of his brother Thomas at Hitchin. Little is known of his last years, but he died, probably poor, in 1634. The fullest account of his life is to be found in Jacquot.[2]

Of all his writings, Chapman undoubtedly took his translations of Homer most seriously. In the opening lines of *The Teares of Peace* he describes how, 'on the hill Next Hitchins' left hand', he had a vision of Homer from which sprang his mission to 'english' the Greek poet; and as the great work progressed we can see Chapman gradually identifying himself with Homer in a manner both sublime and pathetic. Having completed the lesser Homerica and reached 'the end of all the endless works of Homer', he boasts proudly, 'The Worke that I was borne to doe is done'. He turned to the drama presumably to keep the wolf from the door, and his early plays are all comedies which show him to have been a first-rate man of the theatre with an up-to-date knowledge of theatrical fashion. *The Blind Beggar of Alexandria* (1595–6) is a Peele-type fantasy full of Marlovian echoes; *An Humourous Day's Mirth* (1597), in contrast, has a satiric edge and is perhaps the initiator of the play of Humours which Jonson was to develop. *All Fools* (1598–9) and *May Day* (1601–2) show the humanist influence, being imitated from Italian and Terentian comedy;

---

[1] See M. C. Bradbrook, *The School of Night* (C.U.P. 1936), Frances Yates, *A Study of Love's Labour's Lost* (1936) and E. A. Strathmann, *Sir Walter Raleigh*, Columbia, 1951.

[2] Jean Jacquot, *George Chapman*, 1951.

while *The Gentleman Usher* (1601–2) and *Monsieur D'Olive* (1604–5) are in the richer romantic manner of *Twelfth Night*. In yet another mode, the topical comedy, *Eastward Ho* (1605), which he wrote jointly with Jonson and Marston, earned all three a spell in gaol for its satire on James' Scottish followers. His tragedies are topical in a different way, drawing for the most part on recent French history for their subjects. The greatest and most popular, *Bussy D'Ambois* (c. 1604), was followed by the two plays on Biron, *The Conspiracy and Tragedy of Charles, Duke of Biron* (1607–8), whose extreme topicality led to a French protest which caused the plays to be expurgated and drove Chapman from London. Both Bussy and Biron are Marlovian heroes whose greatness comes from the splendour of their passion, although in both cases Chapman shows himself clearly aware of the dangers of excessive passion. In his later tragedies his attitude becomes increasingly didactic and his plays become little more than mouthpieces for his stoicism. The hero of *The Revenge of Bussy D'Ambois* (1610–11) combines with the courage of his brother, Bussy, a quite new self control and indifference to worldly success which makes him more worthy but less dramatic, and the tendency is developed further in *The Tragedy of Chabot* and *Caesar and Pompey* (1612–3). Chapman's tragedies show a sad decline from a complex sense of the conflict in life to an oversimplified and infinitely less dramatic didactism.

THE PLAY

Bussy D'Ambois was entered in the Stationer's Register
3 June 1607 and published in the same year. Elias
Schwartz[1] has argued for an early date—1597—for the
composition of the play, but the general critical opinion
follows Parrott in suggesting 1604 as a more likely date—
an assumption based largely on the topical references to
the old queen, to Leap year and to James' Scottish followers
in Act I, Sc.ii of the play. Parrott[2] suggests that it was
originally written for the Children of the Chapel Royal for
whom Chapman was writing at the time, and who became
Children of the Queen's Revels shortly after. It was then
carried over to the Children of Paul's by the manager,
Kirkham, who transferred in 1605–6, and was 'often presented' by them as the title page to the 1607 Quarto tells
us. It was revised, probably about 1610, to match with its
sequel, *The Revenge of Bussy D'Ambois* and was, at this stage,
associated with the name of Nathaniel Field, the actor and
playwright who managed the Queen's Revels from 1610–16,
and who took it over with him to the King's men for whom
he played the title role until his death in 1619. The prologue
to the play, printed with the Quarto of 1641, is a manifesto
by the King's men vindicating their title to the play in the
1630's when it was still being performed. It was revived at
the Restoration and drew Dryden's censure,[3] and it was
'improved' by D'Urfey in 1691. Since then, it has remained
almost unacted and was generally ignored until Swinburne's
essay in Shepherd's edition of Chapman's plays in 1875.
There have been good texts of the play by Boas (1905),
Parrott (1910), Jacquot (1960) and Lordi (1964). The only
edition with adequate notes, however, is that of Brooke for
the Revels (1964).

All but one of Chapman's tragedies are about contemporary French history, and in using such material, Chapman
had the precedent of Marlowe's *Massacre of Paris* which
included in its cast some of the characters who appear in

[1] Modern Philology, LVII, No. 2. Nov. 1959.

[2] Tragedies of George Chapman.

[3] *Dedication to the Spanish Friar.*

Bussy. The choice of Bussy as subject for a tragedy was not a strange one, for he was a figure well known both on account of his political activities and his amorous exploits. He was also something of a scholar and minor poet, involved in the court circle of Catherine de Medici and Henry III, with their interests in Neo-Platonism and Hermetic magic; and the combination of man of action and of learning must have made a special appeal to a writer of Chapman's temperament. The historical Bussy was at first in the service of Henry III but changed in 1575 to that of the king's brother Alençon, later Anjou, the *Monsieur* of the play. He was for a time governor of the province of Anjou, but earned the king's displeasure by his unruly behaviour. In 1578 he was in Flanders, engaged in negotiations with Walsingham and in plans for the Anjou marriage to Elizabeth. By this time, however, he seems to have offended Anjou as well as the king, so that when he revealed to his patron his success in wooing the wife of the Count Montsoreau, Anjou told Henry of it, who at once betrayed it to the husband. Montsoreau forced his wife at pistol point to summon her lover, and Bussy was killed in an ambush in 1579 at a time when Anjou was in England. The contemporary written accounts of the story, which are fully transcribed in the editions of Boas and Jacquot, were all too late for Chapman to have used for his play, but he could easily have heard of it from Grimestone or picked it up during his travels in the Low Countries. What matters, however, is the dramatic use he made of the story, and it can be seen that although his general conception of Bussy's fiery and adventurous character is true to life, his play departs from the facts in several minor yet significant ways. For example, he makes Bussy poor, which was not the case in real life, and he makes him the centre of a great three-a-side duel resembling one which took place in 1578, but in which Bussy was not actually involved. The significance of these changes will become apparent.

Bussy D'Ambois takes its shape from a variety of sources. On the one hand, as Brooke has shown, it owes much to the tradition of the Morality play; the opening scene might be a debate between Poverty and Riches, and the entry of Bussy Poor, or Bussy, in a New Suit accompanied by two pages, verges at times on allegory. On the other side, with its ghost and blood and classical nuntius, it is perhaps the most Senecan play of the whole period. Chapman, always a self-conscious humanist, inevitably turned to the accepted

authority for his first attempt in the tragic kind, and his
specific model was Seneca's *Hercules Oetaeus*, the play which
described the death of Hercules as a result of the poisoned
shirt of Nessus mistakenly given to him by Dejanira.
Chapman's play abounds in references to Hercules'
labours: Bussy sees himself as a new Hercules sent down to
kill the Hydras and clean out the Augean stables of the
modern world; like Hercules he dies as a result of a love
affair and like him wishes to be made a star; at the point of
death he gives his sword to Montsurry, as the dying
Hercules in Seneca gave his bow and arrows to Philoctetes,
and like Hercules, he dies standing up, leaning to neither
side. As the notes will show, Bussy's dying speeches are a
tissue of echoes and adaptations of Seneca's play, but it is
important to realize that Chapman's play is an 'imitation'
not a copy, and that he takes great liberties with his original
to suit his own literary purposes. For example, he transfers
Dejanira's jealous ravings to Montsurry (V.i, 86), or
changes a relatively unimpassioned speech by Hylas into a
great lament by Tamyra. (V.iii, 210).

The plays of Marlowe are another major literary influence
on *Bussy*. The presence of *Dr. Faustus* can be felt in the
Morality play element and perhaps, too, in the necromancy
of the play, but the influence of *Tamburlaine* is much greater
here and in the plays about Biron which follow it. Chapman's heroes rise, like Tamburlaine, by their own fiery
element and seek to join the stars. Tamburlaine begins by
thinking of himself as Jove's instrument to scourge mankind, but eventually comes to identify himself with Jove
thrusting his 'doting father', Chronos, from the throne and
climbing there in his place, though his enemies see him only
as a presumptuous Titan to be crushed by Jove for his
rebellion. Bussy, too, sees himself as a Jove striking down
the giants, whereas Monsieur thinks of himself as the Jove
and of Bussy as the giant to be 'struck under th'Aetna of his
pride' by the same 'doting' hand which raised him (III.ii,
136). The myths of Jove and the Titans and of Jove and
Chronos run through the two plays giving to both a basic
ambiguity, since we cannot tell in either case whether the
death of the hero marks his ascent to a higher sphere like
Jove or Hercules, or whether it marks his fall for presump-
tion, like the Titans. Bussy lives like a Hercules but dies
like a Titan, only to be promised stellification, however, in
the final speech of the play.

This ambiguity has led to interpretations of *Bussy* which

vary from that of Ennis Rees at the one extreme, who sees
the play as a simple condemnation of unregulated passion,[1]
to that of Hardin Craig,[2] or Elias Schwartz[3] at the other,
who look on Chapman as the champion of the passions, and
on Bussy himself as an eminently virtuous hero. Neither
of these conceptions is adequate: the one ignores the obvious
nobility with which Chapman invests his hero, and the
other Chapman's ethical beliefs as expressed in his other
works. Yet the conflicting interpretations point to a real
problem which the play presents, namely that Bussy appears
to be admired for actions which would normally be censured. As Schwartz says, Bussy is 'both a murderer and an
adulterer. But within the play's ethical context he is seen
as faultless'. Chapman involves him in a love affair which
entails hypocrisy and the corruption of religion; he makes
him fight a pointless and particularly bloody duel—a duel
in which the historical Bussy took no part, so that Chapman's attribution of it to him is calculated; yet he lets him
die heroically without repenting and be held up as a paragon
by his enemies, Monsieur and Guise. Bussy is never
explicitly censured for his actions, and the conflict within
the play is not the traditional one between reason and passion, but between passion and policy in which passion is
clearly the nobler on account of its simplicity and directness.
It is everywhere accepted as being outside the control of
reason: Tamyra's passion for Bussy is as violent and as
irresistible as an earthquake; it has nothing to do with love
and, indeed, coexists with her very real love for her husband,
as she confesses at II.ii, 174; yet the Friar makes no attempt
to check it since

. . . our affections' storm
Raised in the blood, no reason can reform. (II.ii, 187)

Bussy attributes our uncontrollable moods to a 'natural
sickness of the blood', (IV.i, 29) and Monsieur diagnoses the
cause as an unbalance of humours resulting from the fact that
the soul is not 'diffused quite through'. (III.ii, 352). What
Hardin Craig describes as 'a sort of Psychological determinism' in the play is really a physiological determinism

[1] Ennis Rees, *The Tragedies of George Chapman.* (Harvard), 1954.
[2] *The Parrott Presentation Volume,* ed. Hardin Craig. Princeton, 1935, pp. 32–5.
[3] 'Seneca, Homer & Chapman's *Bussy D'Ambois'.* J. E. G. P. 56. 1957.

springing out of the fallen nature of the blood itself, since the Fall corrupted mankind. Blood in its various senses, as a particular humour or as the chariot for our distempered humours through the body, is at the heart of the play and forms the source of Bussy's anger or Tamyra's desire or Montsurry's jealousy alike. "Twas from my troubled blood, and not from me' (IV.i, 153) says Montsurry in explanation of his sudden suspicions, and Chapman makes both literal and symbolic use of blood as the cause, the agent and the result of human actions. Bussy's first act is to give Maffé a bloody crown—'These crowns are sown in blood; blood be their fruit.' (I.i, 220), and the first fruits of Monsieur's crowns are the new clothes which result in the bloody duel with Barrisor, whose blood in turn becomes the pretext for the assignation with Tamyra—. 'Lord Barrisor, whom you slew . . . of all which. . . . She keeps one letter written in his blood' (II.ii, 199), just as at the end it is Tamyra's letter written in her own blood which draws Bussy to his death. Passion springs from the blood and is punished through it in a peculiarly literal way; but Chapman's attitude is not one of simple condemnation such as we find in *The Revenge of Bussy*. He is praising passion as well as condemning it, and his poems help us to understand why, since they contain a direct statement of his beliefs in terms which are frequently echoed in the plays.

Chapman is a Renaissance Neo-Platonist, accepting the traditional hierarchy of mind, soul and body in which the soul forms the intermediary between material and spiritual, able to ascend and be absorbed into mind or to sink and be subdued in matter. The highest human state is that in which mind transcends the body and merges itself in the eternal, the Cynthia of his early poems whose attainment is the object of all human desire. From Cynthia alone comes the true peace of mind, the Euthymiae whose loss is lamented in *Euthymiae Raptus, The Teares of Peace*. The means to achieve this happy state is Learning, by which the mind informs and shapes the soul so that it is capable of keeping the body in its proper place:

> But this is Learning; To have skill to throwe
> Reignes on your bodies powres, that nothing knowe;
> And fill the soules powers, so with act, and art,
> That she can curbe the bodies angrie part: . . .
>   (*Teares of Peace*. Ll. 504–7)

Chapman is never tired of singing the praises of Learning

which he frequently compares to Hercules conquering the monsters of the earth. It is 'Herculean Learning' which overcomes the Hydras of 'unnumbered passions' and the 'Appetites that never will be bridled',[1] and it is relevant to our understanding of *Bussy* that Chapman uses Hercules as a symbol of everything that helps on the nobler life of the spirit. In *The Shadow of Night* he invokes the help of Hercules to 'cleanse this beastly stable of the world' and to shoot his arrow at the sun of worldliness which challenges the reign of Cynthia and contemplation.[2] In *Eugenia* he equates the human body with the shirt of Nessus which 'makes the Noblest that indues it, rave'. (l. 831). Shakespeare uses the same symbolism in *Antony and Cleopatra*, a play having some affinity with *Bussy*, when he makes Antony cry in his tormented passion: 'The shirt of Nessus is upon me'. (IV.x, 56).

The greatest enemy of Learning and of Cynthia is what Chapman in *The Teares of Peace* calls the 'Active' life, which is the pursuit of earthly desires and material ambitions. The 'Active Man' resembles Monsieur, the Guise and in part, Bussy, both for what he is and for the terms used to describe him which so frequently echo the language of *Bussy*. The followers of the active life are

> . . . men of ragges,
> Of Titles meerely, Places, Fortunes, Bragges . . .
> (401–2)

Like Guise they are noble in blood but not in soul; (337) they are 'Giants, throwing goulden hills gainst heaven'; (407) their desires can never be appeased, 'like to Spirits raised/Without a circle' (674–5); they are like beasts whose souls are incapable of ruling 'all the bodies mutinous Realme' (668); they have 'no strength, but weakens them' (676), and eventually they fall from their high places like exhalations 'That would be thought Starres'. (1010).

Chapman never changes his mind about these basic values; from first to last he insists that 'In-sight illustrates; outward braverie blindes'; but he does change his conception of how the good life may best be achieved. In the early poem, *Ovid's Banquet of Sense*, he takes up the orthodox Platonic position as expressed, for example, in the last book of Castiglione's *Courtier*. The lover can transcend the body

[1] *Teares of Peace*, 698

[2] *Hymnus in Noctem* 255.

by means of the body, and using it as a stair, mount from the knowledge of particular beauties to that of the universal beauty. By the time he wrote the *Teares of Peace* and the *Revenge of Bussy D'Ambois*, however, he had turned against the life of the senses, 'This bond and bundle of corruption', and embraced the stoical doctrine of non-attachment embodied in Clermont D'Ambois or Chabot. The change corresponds roughly to the change in his attitude towards Homer which he defines in his dedication to Somerset prefacing the *Odyssey*:

> ... the first word of his Iliads is ... wrath; the first word of his Odysses ... Man. ... In one, Predominant Perturbation; in the other, over-ruling Wisedome; in one, the Bodie's fervour and fashion of outward Fortitude to all possible height of Heroicall Action; in the other, the Mind's inward, constant and unconquered Empire. ...

Bussy and Achilles are heroes of a different order from Clermont and Odysseus, in that their greatness comes from their abandonment to rather than their control of passion, and their affinities are with Chapman's earlier Neo-Platonism rather than with his later stoicism. The kind of relative virtue which is possible through passion is defined by Chapman in his curious allegory of the hunting of Euthimya in his *Hymnus in Cynthiam*, which forms the second part of *The Shadow of Night*. In this poem, Cynthia, the moon, is Chapman's symbol of divinity; her sphere transcends that of the earth and her court has 'everie corner fild/ By Bewtious Forme': (194–5) she is only visible by night when the eyes of the mind are not blinded by the dazzling sun of worldly activities. When the day comes, however, she frames out of the purest matter of earth, 'To wit, a bright, and daseling meteor' (211) a beautiful nymph, Euthimya, who has the power to assume what shape she pleases. Cynthia next creates out of 'the flowrs, the shadowes and the mists' of earth (220) a pack of hounds and a set of huntsmen who, mounted on lions, boars and unicorns, give chase to the nymph. Euthimya first changes herself into a panther and leads the chase into a dark thicket where all are torn and terrified by the thorns and shadows they encounter there, after which she turns herself into a boar and draws them into a beautiful and apparently fruitful island whose fruits are loathed as soon as tasted. So the phantom chase goes on until night falls again and 'Her morns creation did like vapours wast'. (393). This is Chapman's picture of the

One and the Many, celestial and terrestrial: men and the things they desire on earth are only shadows, yet because all are created by Cynthia all contain some of her divinity at however many removes. The panther of worldly ambition and the boar of physical desire which men pursue are really Euthimya, the vision of divinity which all men seek and which reduces itself to the level of comprehension in the material world: 'Wisedome conformes her selfe to all earths guises.' (229). For this reason men will pursue their desires in vain and be eternally tormented by their inability to fulfil them, yet from this, as Chapman points out, wisdom may be learned, though by a roundabout route. The shirt of Nessus purefies by tormenting. 'Eyes should guide bodies and our soules our eyes' (320) he says, but passion works in the contrary way, beginning with the eyes and touching the heart with a pity which should by rights begin in the mind. Nevertheless, the promptings of passion have a relative nobility because they spring from an unconscious desire for the eternal and embody the pursuit of the divine as it appears through its temporal covering. Only Policy is wholly evil since it recognizes nothing beyond the merely physical and makes men content with shadows: it is more at ease and more successful in the world but can never lead to true wisdom.

This is the basis of Chapman's paradoxical attitude to passion in *Bussy D'Ambois*. It is geared to illusions which must fail in the end and yet, in Pero's words, it is 'true fire', even if put 'To a false train, to blow up long crowned peace'. (IV.i, 219). It is noble in comparison with the cynical materialism of the Machiavels yet in absolute terms it is corrupted through the Fall and, like the hunter and the hunted, no more than a shadow of Reality. On the one hand, therefore, Bussy's rash choler and Tamyra's headlong desire are brought into careful contrast with Monsieur's politic friendship and cold-blooded lust and shown to be the nobler. On the other hand, such passions can never find satisfaction: the peace and stillness which Tamyra prays she may find at the heart of her love affair—'this charmed hour/ Fix like the Centre' (II.ii, 165)—are in reality only the beginning of another form of movement:

> . . . the first orb move
> In this our set and cunning world of love. (II.ii, 195)

The outcome is inevitably tragic, yet a tragedy from which true wisdom may spring.

At the beginning of the play Bussy recognizes the futility of the world's desires and their opposition to true virtue:

> Man is a torch borne in the wind: a dream
> But of a shadow, summed with all his substance.
>
> (I.i, 18)

He is, however, as well as a philosopher, a man of the world; a mixture of idealist and malcontent who hopes to have it both ways and rise *with* virtue (I.i, 130). His problem is that of Chapman himself who, as he tells us in his epistle to Harriot, perpetually struggled to escape from 'Under the clawes of this fowle Panther earth', (46) yet was forced to 'make friends/ Of the unrighteous Mammon' (28) because the soul depends upon the flesh. Bussy's compromise with the world at once drags passion down to the level of policy: Tamyra is forced into hypocrisy, Bussy to make unnatural attempts to rival Monsieur at his own game, (IV.ii, 154-) and even the Friar is turned ironically into an advocate of politic ways and double meanings (II.ii, 221). The magic which they attempt is perverted by the passion out of which it springs, so that the supernatural warnings given to them are deceptive, like those given to Faustus or Macbeth, and for the same reason. In this course, the very integrity which is the virtue of their passion becomes a handicap. Bussy's chivalry and sense of Honour draws him to his death, and Tamyra's idealism gives her a harder fate than that of more cynical wives:

> Oh, had I never married but for form,
> Never vowed faith but purposed to deceive,
> Never made conscience of any sin . . .
> Happy had I been then, as others are
> Of the like licence. . . . (V.iii, 219)

The honesty of passion has no chance against policy. This is the point which Chapman debates in the great choric scene between Monsieur and the Guise at the beginning of Act V, Scene iii. The climax is approaching and the two characters, in full knowledge of the tragedy about to be enacted below, debate its significance. Here, says Monsieur, is a man whom Nature has created 'learned, valiant, virtuous and full manned' and whom now she allows to be destroyed because of those very virtues, while emptier creatures live and thrive in the same conditions. Surely, the only reasonable assumption is that Nature has no certain plan in the world, 'Not knowing what she does', and there is no such

thing as divine providence. The Guise cannot accept so
atheistical a point of view: such a belief, he argues, can only
be held by a worldly man who values things merely 'by the
events (V.iii, 26). But the events seem to justify Monsieur's
opinion and Bussy himself dies believing it—'Oh, frail
condition of strength, valour, virtue. . . .' (V.iii, 188).

Chapman, however, thinks differently. Bussy's life ends
in defeat, but defeat has taught him wisdom: he recognizes
in truth now, at the point of death, what he affirmed in
words but denied in his actions at the start of the play, that
life is indeed 'nothing but a courtier's breath' (V.iii, 132).
He becomes capable, therefore, of 'an equal thought . . . of
life and death' (V.iii, 142), a stoical acceptance of his own
failure which the sight of Tamyra's wounds serves to
intensify. Of even greater significance, however, is the
return of the Friar as a ghost whose very presence, charged
with the task of repairing some of the evil he has helped to
cause, is proof of some sort of divine providence. Moreover,
the morality which he preaches is the converse of that which
has dominated the play: against violence, jealousy, lust and
selfish Honour is set a creed of love, forgiveness and order.
It is the same love which Peace bore in a coffin and mourned
for in *The Teares of Peace*—'Man's want of Peace, which was
from want of love' (148)—and Bussy accepts its validity in
his dying moments when he forgives his murderers and
urges Montsurry to be reconciled with Tamyra. There can,
of course, be no simple happy ending with a sudden change
of heart. Chapman is very clear that the world is a fallen
place, and the long emblem of the candle which retains a
spice of its first parents till, like Adam, 'it sees and dies'
(V.iii, 257) insists on the final disharmony of Tamyra and
Montsurry and of life itself. Montsurry remains a 'son of the
earth' and Bussy's spirit must leave his body before it can
escape from the sphere of the four elements and burn its
way upwards to the celestial sphere.

This is a part but not, I think, the whole of Chapman's
meaning in the Friar's final speech which has some puzzling
features, and I quote it in full:

Farewell, brave relicts of a complete man;
Look up and see thy spirit made a star;
Join flames with Hercules, and when thou settest
Thy radiant forehead in the firmament
Make the vast continent, cracked with thy receipt,
Spread to a world of fire, and th' aged sky
Cheer with new sparks of old humanity.

(V.iii, 268–)

The body remains below and the spirit ascends to a higher
and purer sphere—that is orthodox Christianity or Platonism. But why should the firmament, which comprised the
spheres of the planets and the fixed stars, be set on fire; and
why should the aged sky be cheered or need cheering by the
ascent of Bussy's virtue? Brooke takes the word 'continent'
to refer to the sphere of the moon, the outer bound of the
corrupted elements since the Fall, and suggests that Bussy's
breaking through it symbolizes a return to man's prelapsarian communication with the heavens.'The significance
which (the Friar) attached to Bussy's death', he continues,
'is not just that one man goes to heaven, but that in his
example all mankind may see a—remote—hope of escape
from the fallen world.'[1] I would suggest that Chapman's
meaning in this passage is more specific, and that he is
referring to a work of the Italian writer Giordano Bruno,
namely his *Spaccio della bestia Trionfante*, 'The expulsion
of the triumphant Beast', which was dedicated to Sidney in
1585. Bruno came to London in 1583 from the court of
Henry III of France—the Henry of *Bussy D'Ambois*. He was
a notorious figure quickly involved in public controversy
and, as Frances Yates[2] has shown, was associated with the
group of advanced thinkers surrounding Raleigh with whom
Chapman was familiar. His works written in England were
widely read: his *Eroici Furori* was immensely influential on
the Elizabethan love sonnet, and his *Spaccio* was still well
enough known in 1634 for Carew to base on it his masque,
Coelum Britannicum. The *Spaccio* seems to contain many
parallels with *Bussy* and to throw light on its interpretation.
It deals with a reformation of the heavens: Jove holds a
banquet for the planetary deities on the anniversary of his
conquest of the giants. He is old and impotent and lament-
ably in need of cheering because men no longer worship the
stellar deities as they used to. The reason is that the constellations have become associated with all the vices of the gods
instead of with their virtues; they have either taken the
names of beasts, such as the Ram or the Bear, or else they
commemorate the delinquencies or at least the less god-like
escapades of the gods. Chapman refers to the same thing in
his *Hymnus in Noctem*, when he writes:

> Kinde Amalthaea was transferd by Jove,
> Into his sparckling pavement, for her love,

---

[1] Revels, p. 144–5 note.

[2] *Giordano Bruno and the Hermetic tradition* (Routledge 1964).

Though but a Goate, and giving him her milke
(105–)

Even Hercules who rose to the stars on account of his merit
is still a testimony of his father's lechery. Jove suggests,
therefore, that the heavens shall be purged of their vices so
that the 'constellations and influxes shall be new', and he
goes through the forty-eight constellations, casting down the
vices associated with them and elevating the appropriate
virtues in their place. Thus Truth, Justice, Prudence, Law,
Concord take up their places in the Great Bear, Scorpio,
Bootes and the Pleiades, driving out Fraud, Treason,
Crime, Faction, and so on. Hercules, too, has to go, but
because of his intrinsic worth he is sent down to earth to
slay the modern monsters, just as Bussy feels it is his task
to do. On his departure, Riches and Poverty apply for his
place in the heavens—Riches because she is what all men
desire; Poverty, because she is the opposite of Riches. Jove
denies that Riches is a virtue; she is the servant of good and
bad alike but is more likely to gravitate to the bad: equally,
poverty is not a virtue since she enviously dogs the steps of
riches. Avarice is the shadow of both, and the only true
virtue is the contentment which comes with the absence of
desire. Jove therefore refuses both a place in heaven. When
they have gone, Fortune rises to demand the empty place of
Hercules, but she, too, is denied a place among the stars,
although Jove hands over the whole sub-lunar sphere to
her charge. She departs, therefore, preceded by Occasion
and accompanied by Riches and Poverty with all their train
of joys and sorrows, to take up her rule on earth, and the
place of Hercules in heaven is given to Fortitude. This is a
conventional enough conception, but it comes very close to
the situation of Bussy. In the opening sequence of the play
he complains of living in a world dominated by Fortune,
but he mistakes his poverty for a virtue because it is the
opposite of riches and then seeks to make riches a virtue,
when Monsieur provides the occasion. He does not fully
realize until the end of the play that neither is a virtue in a
world where all is worthless. The similarity to Bruno's
parable, combined with the fact that Bussy is coupled with
Hercules, suggests that Chapman had the *Spaccio* in mind.
The most significant parallel, however, lies in the scheme of
reformation for the heavens, for the virtues which Jove
proposes to introduce are essentially those which Bussy
brings with him at his ascent. They are the justice and
observance of Nature's law which Henry admires in Bussy

at III, ii, 90– and which he sees as relics of the Golden Age,
before the things of nature had been given over 'unjustly to
the hand of Fortune'. They are also the love, charity, forgiveness and magnanimity which the Friar's ghost advocates
and which Bussy embraces at the end. Jove's great vision of
a regenerated heaven is based on the acceptance of all the
virtues which Bussy possesses by nature or learns by suffering, and the rejection of all the lusts, dissensions, violence
and deceit of the world of Fortune and greatness in which
Monsieur prospers.

Bruno tells us the meaning of his myth in his Preface to
Sidney. He accepts the traditional conception that man is
the microcosm of the whole universe and that his threefold
hierarchy of body, soul and mind corresponds to the different levels of the whole creation. The mind of man is of the
same essence as the stars and the one portrays the other.
There is in every man, he says, a whole world, a universe,
and the stellar Gods of his parable therefore symbolize the
virtues and powers of the human soul. Under cover of his
reform of the heavens, in fact, Bruno is really advocating a
reform of earth and a new code of human values. The full
significance of this has been suggested by Frances Yates,[1]
and is very relevant to our study of Chapman. Bruno, like
many Renaissance thinkers, was a Hermetic, believing in
what he took to be the religion of the ancient Egyptians
from which both Christianity and Platonism were thought
to be derived. The source of these beliefs was a number of
Greek treatises written by Christian-Platonist mystics of
the second century A.D. but mistakenly attributed by the
Renaissance to the entirely mythological figure, Hermes
Trismegisthus, who, it was thought, lived before either
Plato or Moses and from whom they derived their wisdom.
Bruno equated this ancient religion and its civilization with
the Golden Age when virtue, love and peace prevailed,
before subsequent religions had clouded the original truths
and embroiled the world in religious sects and dissensions.
Magic formed a serious part of the Hermetic philosophy,
but of a nobler kind than the necromancy of the middle ages
or of Faust or Bussy's Friar. Because men were virtuous,
they could exploit those aspects of the stars which corres-
ponded to their virtues, and control all the spiritual hier-
archies, both good and evil, without danger. Thus their
virtue, based on a true religion and a divine magic, streng-
thened and perpetuated itself. Such a belief appealed to

[1] Op. cit. Chap. XI–XIII.

Renaissance idealism and seemed to offer an escape from the mounting tide of religious intolerance and persecution which stemmed from the Reformation. Bruno turned to it for this reason, but also encouraged particularly by the new Copernican cosmology, which placed the sun in the centre of the universe, instead of the earth as in the Ptolemaic scheme. He saw this as heralding the re-birth of the ancient Egyptian sun-worship and with it a new Golden age of peace, love and virtue. This is what he is prophesying and pleading for in the *Spaccio*—a new virtue and a new use of the stellar influences made possible by it; and I think that Chapman, who moved in circles very familiar with these ideas, must have understood his intention. Bussy's time-honoured virtues are those of the Golden Age, but his mod-ern vices make him incapable of distinguishing between the true magic of Apollo, the sun god, and the deceiving magic of his infernal equivalent, Behemoth, Prince of shades; in his hour of need he invokes the help of both indiscriminately (V.ii, 39–51). The Hermetist would attribute this to the blindness of a world which has lost its ancient wisdom.

It is impossible to say how far Chapman believed in Bruno's Hermeticism or whether he associated it with the Copernican revolution, although he refers to the earth's movement on several occasions.[1] There is much in his poetry, however, which indicates the Hermetic influence. To Chapman, Poetry was always something cabalistic, hiding within its outer rind, holy mysteries to which only the initiated, those with what he called 'light-bearing intellect', could penetrate. The 'Learning' which he venerates but never defines seems to imply a mystical knowledge of the divine truths which he believes to lie at the heart of Homer's tales, and Chapman is a staunch defender and practiser of allegory. Learning is the key to the wisdom of the golden age and the means by which the ancient virtues may be recovered, a recovery which he describes in terms echoing the 'new sparks of old humanity' prophesied by the friar:

> Let all men judge; who is it can denie,
> That the rich crowne of ould Humanitie,
> Is still your birth-right? and was ne're let downe
> From heaven, for rule of Beasts lives but your owne?
> *(Teares of Peace, 564)*

---

[1] *Bussy* v. I, 153. *The Teares of Peace*, 215–16.

All this is in the Hermetic mode, and I would suggest, therefore, that in *Bussy D'Ambois*, Chapman is writing his own *Spaccio*: he is showing the expulsion of the triumphant beast of the vices and prophesying their replacement by the ancient virtues. As in his *Teares of Peace* he is pleading for peace on several levels, for the contentment of mind, the Euthymiae which only Cynthia can give, and for the social peace and harmony which comes from an ethic based on love instead of on self-interest and the niceties of honour. The parallel must not, of course, be pushed too far; Chapman was writing a tragedy not a pamphlet, and he was in any case of a more sombre temperament than Bruno. *Bussy* is as much an expression of despairing hope as an attempt at prophecy, and Chapman grew more pessimistic as he became older. It is because the play achieves a precarious balance between a sense of man's Fall and of his potentialities that it can combine pettiness and heroism, cruelty and idealism in a single tragic whole. There is no play outside those of Shakespeare in the period which is so many-sided.

Bussy D'Ambois, then, is a good deal more than a play about contemporary history; it is at once a record of Chapman's own personal struggles in a world hostile to his idealism, and a statement of his deepest hopes for the future of mankind. He is more deeply involved in it than in any of his other plays, and for this reason the poetry is of unrivalled complexity and passion. The main themes are reflected and reinforced by a network of interwoven images which creates a world in which the action of the play seems both logical and inevitable. Guise compares the orderless world of Monsieur's atheism to a statue carved perfectly up to the neck but left without a head (V.iii, 30): to a religious man, Nature would be incapable of such indecorum. But the world appears to run by Monsieur's values, and Chapman indicates its monstrosity by repeated images of physical deformity: 'Reward goes backward, Honour on his head'; Flattery with his legs wrapped round with 'Kings' soothed guts'; Bussy rising upwards like an Atlas under the King's arm, or Montsurry's grotesque picture of the world turning over and exposing her diseased back parts. In a world such as this, the animality of Bussy's duel or the monstrosity of Tamyra's wracking seem natural. Although, ironically, Bussy fails to realize that his own course of action has involved him in the same unnatural pattern, he is nevertheless the only character in the play who recognizes the source of the evil. He sees that virtue and greatness are hostile to one another in the world, and that virtue is the reality, greatness merely the shadow. This contrast between appearance and reality, external show and inner worth, is reflected with extraordinary consistency by the imagery throughout. The first line of the play sets the pattern of the conflict:

Fortune, not Reason, rules the state of things

and this is developed through an infinite variety of contrasts between real and unreal worth, the empty and the full man, the solid and the merely inflated. Bussy talks of the 'tympanous statists' resembling hollow statues stuffed only with mortar, flint and lead (I.i, 10–); he varies the image when he attacks the great man who 'Bombasts his private roofs with public riches' (III.ii, 27); and Monsieur echoes it when he contrasts the 'lean darkness' of private virtue with the banquet of Fortune (I.i, 62), or the hollow tree, which remains standing because its emptiness lets the wind blow through it, with the solid tree which, like Bussy, is blown down (V.iii, 42–). The same contrast, in different terms, is made between the greatness of Guise, which lies in his 'faction' or in his 'blood' with all the ambiguity the word implies, and that of Bussy which lies in his merit. 'He has more titles', says Monsieur, to which Bussy retorts in true Herculean style, 'So Hydra had more heads' (III.ii, 74). The effect of such a background of imagery is to underline the moral values of the play and to invest the action itself with symbolism. Fine clothes, for example, offer themselves as an image of this merely outward greatness, and Chapman associates them with it:

Brave barks and outward gloss
Attract court eyes, be in-parts ne'er so gross. (I.i, 110)

In consequence, Bussy's acquisition of a new suit becomes a constant and ironic reminder that he has succumbed to the very values he is attacking, and the duel which his new suit immediately precipitates becomes a symbolic retribution for his descent to court values and passions. It is equally symbolic that he is deceived by Montsurry's assumption of the friar's outward garment; through his involvement in 'Greatness', Bussy can no longer distinguish between appearance and reality.

These image patterns reflect the world in which the action takes place: the metaphysical explanation of this state of things is embodied in a further, most important sequence of images connected with 'exhalations' and derived ultimately from Aristotle's *Meteorologica*. Exhalations were the vapours

drawn up by the heat of the sun, those from the water being
moist and cool, those from the earth, hot and dry. From the
former came clouds and mists; from the latter, earthquakes
if they became imprisoned in the earth, thunder if trapped
in a cloud, hurricanes and winds if they met an obstruction.
The hot and dry exhalations rose by their own nature to
form the element of fire of which the highest layer of the
terrestrial sphere was composed, and this, when heated by
the friction of the rotating lunar sphere which enclosed it,
ignited to produce meteors, comets and shooting stars. All,
however, took their being from the earth; and these fiery
yet earth-bound vapours in their several manifestations
provided Chapman with his central symbol for the passions.
Bussy's fury in the great duel, for example, is compared to
thunder:

> Sorrow and fury, like two opposite fumes
> Met in the upper region of a cloud . . .
> Brake from the earth . . . (II.i, 110)

his terrible anger against Monsieur, to storm and lightning:

> I'll make th'inspired threshals of his court
> Sweat with the weather of my horrid steps. . . .
> A politician must like lightning melt
> The very marrow, and not print the skin: (IV.ii, 163)

For the same reason Tamyra's headlong passion is compared to an earthquake:

> . . . . . as when a fume
> Hot, dry and gross, within the womb of earth . . .
> The more it is compressed, the more it rageth . . .
> And then it tosseth temples in the air, . . . (II.ii, 34)

or again, with more explicit symbolism, she describes the
passions in terms of the clouds which obscure the very sun
which drew them up:

> Our bodies are but thick clouds to our souls
> Through which they cannot shine when they desire.
> When all the stars, and even the sun himself,
> Must stay the vapours' times that he exhales . . .
> Oh, how can we, that are but motes to him . . .
> Disperse our passions' fumes, with our weak labours,
> That are more thick and black than all earth's vapours?
> (III.i, 59)

It is especially ironical, therefore, that Tamyra invokes the
'silently-gliding exhalations' (II.ii, 159) to help produce a

still centre of unearthly peace for her love affair when, by their very nature, they are bound to destroy it. And when Bussy in his bitter moment of self-knowledge finally understands the delusions of passion, it is inevitable that he should describe himself in terms of a falling star which, for all its fiery brilliance, must still sink back to the earth from which it came—'An exhalation that would be a star.' (*Byron's Tragedy*, IV.ii, 292). It is in the context of these images that Bussy's desire to become a fixed star must be read and its symbolism understood. In this last scene of the play, the ascent of Hercules to the stars, the burning shirt of Nessus, the storms and passions of earth and its vapours, all come together to produce a moment of extraordinarily complex and unifying symbolism.

The effect of this subtle interrelation of image and action is to add a dimension which lifts the whole level of the play almost to that of mythology. *Bussy D'Ambois* is not the tragedy of a single man but of mankind; it is not tragedy resulting from an avoidable error but something inescapably built in to human nature since the Fall. Yet Bussy's fall contributes to his greatness: the passions which bring him down also enable him to 'join flames with Hercules' as his more rational brother, Clermont, could never have done. One of the last constellations which the Gods discuss in the *Spaccio* is the Centaur, 'this man that is planted in a beast . . . this beast that is engrafted on a man, in which one person is made up of two natures.' It is significant that Jove allows Chiron to keep his place in the heavens and be a priest at the heavenly altar. In this role he will be a perpetual moral fable, always sacrificing the beast in himself, yet always having the beast within to sacrifice. The tragedy and the justification of Bussy stems from a similar conception of human nature.

THE TEXT

The play exists in two versions. The first, (A), is the
quarto printed for William Aspley in 1607 and again without
alteration in 1608, bearing on its title page 'As it hath been
often presented at Paules.' Stage directions are few, and
characters are apt to be listed en bloc at the beginning of the
scene instead of at their point of entry, suggesting that this
quarto may have been printed from the original manuscript.
The second is the quarto, (B), printed by A.N. for Robert
Lunne in 1641, seven years after Chapman's death. The
title page bears the inscription: 'As it hath been often Acted
with great Applause. Being much corrected and amended by
the Author before his death.' The second quarto is based
on the first, reproducing the spelling and, with a few exceptions, the punctuation of A. It has, however, fuller stage
directions and is altered and emended extensively, suggesting that its ultimate source was a printed prompt copy which
was then systematically worked over at some intervening
period. It has a prologue and epilogue apparently composed
in the 1630's by someone other than Chapman. The most
detailed and illuminating account of the text is to be found
in the Revels edition of the play.

The two quartos differ significantly from each other.
There are, in the first place, a large number of changes of
words or phrases for which there is no discernible motive
and which have no appreciable effect: 'continual storms' for
'incessant storms', 'the rude Scythians' for 'the old Scythians', etc. Some consistent patterns of change can, however,
be seen. For example, the emender seems to have disliked
the repetitious use of words and to have gone through the
play striking out words used a second time in close proximity
to the first: in this way, 'world' used at I.i, 23 is changed to
'earth' eight lines later; the second 'be ruled' at I.i, 117
becomes 'be wise', the 'Hermean rod' at III.ii, 108 and 117
is varied by 'the Hermean virtue'. The revisions of this
kind are often mechanical and ignore dramatic effects made
possible by a calculated use of repetition. The delicate
irony of Bussy's phrasing as he humours Tamyra's pretence
of modesty—'. . . that your conscience / Was *something*
troubled with a false report / That Barrisor's blood should

something touch your hand.' (II.ii, 271)—is destroyed in B by the substitution of 'made some deep scruple with a false report'; and similarly, the contempt in Monsieur's advice to 'court our greatest ladies' greatest women' is lost in 'our greatest ladies' chiefest women'. (III.ii, 160). This attention to the local verbal detail at the expense of the wider dramatic effect is a characteristic of the changes in the later quarto. Occasionally, for example, the emender tightens up a metaphor and makes it more accurate; Maffé's warning, 'These crowns are *sown* in blood; blood be their fruit.' (I.i, 220) is related more accurately to fruit trees by the substitution of 'set' for 'sown', but in the change, the echoes of Bussy's earlier reference to sowing and seed crowns are lost. (I.i, 120). Again, he changes obscure or colloquial or clumsy uses of words wherever he sees them, irrespective of any special dramatic function the original form may have had. The 'tympanous statists' of I.i, 10 become the 'men merely great' of B, a phrase quite as effective and a good deal clearer but no longer forming a part of the imagery of 'inflation' with which greatness is associated throughout the play. Similarly, Bussy's remark about pleasing 'portly ladies With a good carriage' gains in precision but loses in innuendo when 'portly' is changed to 'humorous' (I.i, 92); and his attack on Sin as a monster kept only to show men for 'goddess money' is made less clumsy by the substitution of 'servile money' but at the cost of a radical change in meaning. (III.i, 26). Obviously one of the emender's main intentions was to make the sense immediately clearer; he tidies up awkward lines or adds a line to clarify the meaning of a difficult passage, as, for example, in the complicated comparison between man and woman, sun and moon at the beginning of Act IV, which he pulls together by a new line at the end—'So then they rule in men, not men in them.' (IV.i, 20). In a similar way, he tries to make the dramatic situation more explicit and inform the audience more precisely of motive and plot. In A, for example, the first arrival of Bussy and the Friar through the vault is announced by Tamyra briefly and without explanation:

> See, see, the gulf is opening that will swallow
> Me and my fame for ever . . . (II.ii, 177)

The very brevity of the account allows the use of 'gulf' in a symbolic as well as a literal sense. In B, however, the description becomes at once more detailed and more literal:

> See, see, a vault is opening that was never
> Known to my lord and husband, nor to any
> But him that brings the man I love, and me.

Additions of this kind are very common in B and show, as
Brooke has argued, that the emender was more concerned
with plot, the relationship of characters to each other and
with the theatre itself than was Chapman in A. Certainly
some of the changes result from the direct pressure of the
theatre on the play and reveal a new knowledge of both the
dramatic weaknesses and potentialities of the first version.
New and more dramatic openings are given to scenes, as in
III.i and V.i, for example: non-speaking characters are
given lines or removed altogether, and awkward pauses are
bridged by dialogue, as between IV.i and IV.ii while Tamyra
writes her letter. In addition, scenes and characters in A
which show the possibility of further dramatic exploitation
are developed at length, especially if they have comic
potentialities. Maffé has his scene with Bussy expanded in
I.i, and a new comic scene with Monsieur added in III.ii,
while more is made of Bussy's courtship of the Duchess
(I.ii) and Tamyra's rather ludicrous hypocrisy in III.i.
Finally, the later version makes alterations in the order of
the scenes, particularly in Act V. In A, Monsieur and the
Guise are withdrawn from the action and used as a depersonalized chorus to comment on the meaning of Bussy's
death, which they do from above at the time of its occur-
rence. In B, their discussion is set a scene earlier and they
themselves are brought down to the level of the other characters, made co-plotters with Montsurry and finally given
exit lines, their choric quality being removed in the process. The friar's speech comparing Bussy to Hercules with
which the first version of the play ends is, in the later one,
shortened and moved earlier to the moment of Bussy's
death, and the play is now made to end with the long parting
scene between Montsurry and Tamyra. This was presumably designed to lead more naturally into the sequel, *The
Revenge of Bussy D'Ambois*, which opens with Montsurry
and Tamyra together again, and for the production of which
Bussy may have been revised in the first place.

It can be seen that the revisions in the 1641 quarto are
very extensive, but their effect on the nature of the play is
even greater than their numbers would suggest. They do
in effect turn *Bussy D'Ambois* from one kind of a play to a
totally different one. The first version is in many ways a
Faustus-like play, based on great and simple contrasts

between riches and poverty, passion and policy, and omitting all but the most necessary dramatic details. The revised version, in contrast, is a play of more sophisticated dramatic technique, more in the manner of Massinger or Beaumont and Fletcher. Moreover, the A version is, as I have argued earlier, a play of ideas in which character, structure and imagery are all subordinated to the central purpose. In B, on the other hand, the central control is weakened and the constituent elements tend to fly apart. The imagery is less closely integrated with the central themes, the characters become more individualized and lose something of their semi-allegorical quality; the comedy breaks loose from the restraint of tragic decorum, and the debate of ideas becomes submerged under dramatic situation. This development seems to me to be contrary to Chapman's general development in his later plays and poems which is increasingly towards the unequivocal expression of ideas. For these reasons, therefore, I have accepted the quarto of 1607 as authentic.

What then of the claims of the 1641 quarto to be corrected and amended by the author before his death? Until recently, editors have, with occasional reservations, accepted the version of 1641: Dilke (1814), Boas (1905), Parrot (1910), Jacquot (1960) all based their texts on B. In 1951, however, Berta Sturman[1] challenged its validity, pointing out that it was published by a rather disreputable printer in an irregular, perhaps illegal, way shortly after the original copy-holder, William Aspley, had died. She claimed, therefore, that the publisher's claims for his text could be discounted. Professor Ure replied in defence of the B version in 1953.[2] From a very complete analysis of the emendation, he drew attention to the preponderance of apparently pointless alterations to the text, what he aptly called 'an anxious fidgeting with the text'. He argued that only the author himself would go through the play with such care and bother to make so many changes of so little significance; and he suggested, therefore, that Chapman revised his play for revival at the time of the *Revenge of Bussy*, possibly with advice from Nathaniel Field.

[1] 'The 1641 Edition of Chapman's *Bussy D'Ambois*' (Huntington Library Quarterly, XIV, 1950–1.)

[2] 'Chapman's "Tragedy of Bussy D'Ambois": Problems of the Revised Quarto.' *Modern Language Review*, XLVIII, July 1953. No. 3.

The most recent and revolutionary approach to the play is that of Nicholas Brooke in the Revels edition (1964). Brooke points out that the emendations in the later version are not all of a kind and that, although some are clearly in the manner of Chapman, others are clearly not. He argues, therefore, that the quarto of 1607 underwent revision by more than one hand; that Chapman himself worked over the prompt copy of A, and that a second person emended the play further for revival, copying out the whole play anew in the process. His candidate for this second revision is again Field who was a dramatist himself, having written a play, *A Woman is a Weathercock*, for which Chapman wrote commendatory verses addressed 'To his loved sonne, Nat. Field' in 1612. Field would have Chapman's blessing in the task and would, moreover, have known the play very well from having acted in it. He may therefore have written out much of the play from memory, and the fidgeting which Ure takes to be the sign of an author scrupulous about his own work may simply be the result of slips of memory. Brooke therefore bases his text on A with only three emendations from B which he finds too unmistakably in the style of Chapman to omit.

Brooke's evidence in favour of a double revision of the play seems to me irrefutable, but it is impossible to say in every case which emendations are by Chapman and which by another hand. Many of them are so characteristic of Chapman's style that it is difficult to conceive of their being written by anyone else; yet some of the finest emendations occur in passages of revision that are alien to Chapman's methods and go against the general tenor of the play. It is tempting to include as Chapman's everything which seems good, but such a text could have no authority. I have therefore followed Brooke in using A, but have included from B four passages for whose introduction the internal evidence seems specific and overwhelming. I have indicated their presence by brackets and attempted to justify their inclusion in the notes. All other emendations are given in the appendix. My basic copy-text was McIlwraith's reprint of Parrott which I have emended to correspond with the 1607 quarto. The spelling and punctuation are modernized, and the stage directions are based on the fuller ones of 1641 as emended by Parrott.

FURTHER READING

Editions

Bartlett, P. B.	The Poems of George Chapman. New York, 1941
Boas, F. S.	*Bussy D'Ambois* and *The Revenge of Bussy D'Ambois*, 1905
Brooke, N. S.	*Bussy D'Ambois*. The Revels Plays. Methuen, 1964
Jacquot, J.	*Bussy D'Amboise*. Collection Bilingue des Classiques. Aubier. Paris. 1960
Lordi, R. J.	*Bussy D'Ambois*. Regents Renaissance Drama Series. London. 1964.
Nicoll, A.	Chapman's Homer. Vol. I. *The Iliad* Vol. II. *The Odyssey and Lesser Homerica*. London, 1957
Parrott, T. M.	The Tragedies of Chapman, 1910 The Comedies of Chapman, 1914

Books

Jacquot, J.	*George Chapman*. Paris, 1951
Lord, G. de F.	*The Homeric Renaissance*. Chatto, 1956
MacLure, Millar.	*George Chapman: a critical study*. University of Toronto. 1966.
Rees, E.	*The Tragedies of George Chapman*. Harvard, 1954
Ribner, I.	*Jacobean Tragedy*. Methuen, 1962
Ure, P. ed. J. C. Maxwell.	*Elizabethan and Jacobean Drama. Critical Essays*. Liverpool. 1974
Waith, E. M.	*The Herculean Hero*. Chatto, 1962
Wieler, J. W.	*George Chapman. The effect of Stoicism upon his Tragedies*. New York, 1949
Yates, F.	*Giordano Bruno* and *the Hermetic tradition*, Routledge, 1964

Articles

Battenhouse, R. W.	'Chapman and the Nature of Man.' In *Elizabethan Drama*. Modern Essays in Criticism, ed. R. J. Kaufman. Galaxy Books, 1961

Ferguson, A. S.	'The Plays of George Chapman.' Modern Language Review. XIII. 1918
Muir, E.	'Chapman.' Essays in Literature and Society, 1949
Perkinson, R. H.	'Nature and the Tragic Hero in Chapman's Bussy Plays.' Modern Language Quarterly. 3. 1942
Schwartz, E.	'Seneca, Homer & Chapman's Bussy D'Ambois.' Journal of English and Germanic Philology. 56. 1957
Smalley, D.	'The Ethical bias of Chapman's Homer.' Studies in Philology 36. 1939
Smith, J.	'George Chapman.' Scrutiny IV. 1935–36
Spens, J.	'Chapman's Ethical Thought.' Essays & Studies by members of the English Ass. XI. 1925

DISTRIBUTION OF NOTES

Notes of lexical and immediately explanatory character are usually printed at the foot of the page. Points requiring fuller explanation, together with other supplementary material, will be found at the back.

Bussy D'Ambois:

A
TRAGEDIE:

As

it hath been often presented
at Paules.

LONDON,
Printed for *William Aspley.*
1607.

Buſſy D'Ambois

A
TRAGEDIE:

As it hath been often Acted with
great Applauſe.

Being much corrected and amended
by the Author before his death.

LONDON
Printed by *A.N.* for *Robert Lunne.*
1 6 4 1.

DRAMATIS PERSONAE

Henry III. King of France.
Monsieur. His brother.
The Duke of *Guise.*
The Count of *Montsurry.*
Bussy D'Ambois.
Barrisor,
L'Anou, } Courtiers; enemies of Bussy.
Pyrhot,
Brisac,
Melynell, } Courtiers; friends of Bussy.
Beaumond. An attendant on the King.
Comolet. A Friar.
Maffé. Steward to Monsieur.
Nuntius.
Murderers.
Behemoth,
Cartophylax, } Spirits.
Ghost of the Friar.
Elenor. Duchess of Guise.
Tamyra. Countess of Montsurry.
Beaupré. Niece to Elenor.
Annable. Maid to Elenor.
Pero. Maid to Tamyra.
Charlotte. Maid to Beaupré.
Pyrha. A court lady.
Courtiers. Ladies. Pages. Servants. Spirits, etc.

PROLOGUE

Not out of confidence that none but we
Are able to present this tragedy,
Nor out of envy at the grace of late
It did receive, nor yet to derogate
5   From their deserts, who give out boldly that
They move with equal feet on the same flat;
Neither for all, nor any of such ends,
We offer it, gracious and noble friends,
To your review; we, far from emulation
10   (And, charitably judge, from imitation)
With this work entertain you, a piece known,
And still believed in Court to be our own.
To quit our claim, doubting our right or merit,
Would argue in us poverty of spirit
15   Which we must not subscribe to: Field is gone,
Whose action first did give it name, and one
Who came the nearest to him, is denied
By his gray beard to show the height and pride
Of D'Ambois' youth and bravery; yet to hold
20   Our title still a-foot, and not grow cold
By giving it o'er, a third man with his best
Of care and pains defends our interest;
As Richard he was liked, nor do we fear
In personating D'Ambois he'll appear
25   To faint, or go less, so your free consent,
As heretofore, give him encouragement.

15 Field, Nathaniel Field. See Introduction p. xi.
21 A third man: perhaps Elliard Swanston.

6

Seems honourable. (handwritten)

BUSSY D'AMBOIS

Act I, Scene i

story of his life! (handwritten)

Enter BUSSY D'AMBOIS, *poor.*

Bussy. Fortune, not Reason, rules the state of things,
Reward goes backwards, Honour on his head;
Who is not poor, is monstrous; only Need
Gives form and worth to every human seed.
As cedars beaten with incessant storms,   5
So great men flourish; and do imitate
Unskilful statuaries, who suppose,
In forging a Colossus, if they make him
Straddle enough, strut, and look big, and gape,
Their work is goodly: so our tympanous statists   10
In their affected gravity of voice,
Sourness of countenance, manners' cruelty,
Authority, wealth, and all the spawn of Fortune,
Think they bear all the kingdom's worth before them;
Yet differ not from those colossic statues,   15
Which, with heroic forms without o'er-spread,
Within are nought but mortar, flint, and lead.
Man is a torch borne in the wind; a dream
But of a shadow, summed with all his substance;
And as great seamen, using all their powers   20
And skills in Neptune's deep invisible paths,
In tall ships richly built and ribbed with brass,
To put a girdle round about the world,
When they have done it, coming near their haven,
Are glad to give a warning-piece, and call   25
A poor staid fisherman, that never passed
His country's sight, to waft and guide them in;
So when we wander furthest through the waves
Of glassy Glory and the gulfs of State,

1–80 (see p. 79)   2 *on his head* upside down
3 *Need* poverty   7 *statuaries* makers of statues
10 (see p. 79)   19 (see p. 79)
25 *give a warning-piece* fire a signal gun
27 *waft* convey safely

7

30   Topt with all titles, spreading all our reaches,
        As if each private arm would sphere the world,
        We must to Virtue for her guide resort,
        Or we shall shipwrack in our safest port.

                                         He lies down.

              [*Enter*] MONSIEUR *with two* PAGES.

        Monsieur. There is no second place in numerous state
35   That holds more than a cipher; in a king
        All places are contained. His words and looks
        Are like the flashes and the bolts of Jove;
        His deeds inimitable, like the sea
        That shuts still as it opes, and leaves no tracts
40   Nor prints of precedent for poor men's facts.
        There's but a thread betwixt me and a crown;
        I would not wish it cut, unless by nature;
        Yet to prepare me for that likely fortune,
        'Tis fit I get resolved spirits about me.
45   I followed D'Ambois to this green retreat,
        A man of spirit beyond the reach of fear,
        Who, discontent with his neglected worth,
        Neglects the light, and loves obscure abodes;
        But he is young and haughty, apt to take
50   Fire at advancement, to bear state and flourish;
        In his rise therefore shall my bounties shine:
        None loathes the world so much, nor loves to scoff it,
        But gold and grace will make him surfeit of it.

                        [*Approaching* BUSSY.]
        What, D'Ambois?
        Bussy.   He, sir.
        Monsieur.   Turned to earth, alive?
        Up man, the sun shines on thee.
55   *Bussy.*   Let it shine.
        I am no mote to play in't, as great men are.
        Monsieur. Thinkest thou men great in state, motes in the
            sun?
        They say so that would have thee freeze in shades,
        That, like the gross Sicilian gourmandist,
60   Empty their noses in the cates they love,

      30 *spreading . . . reaches* putting on all canvas   34 (see p. 79)
      39–40 (see p. 79)   44 *resolved* resolute
      50 *to bear state* to hold high position with appropriate splendour
      53 *surfeit* to indulge in to excess
      59 *gourmandist* glutton (see also p. 79)   60 *cates* delicacies

That none may eat but they. Do thou but bring
Light to the banquet Fortune sets before thee,
And thou wilt loathe lean darkness like thy death.
Who would believe thy mettle could let sloth
Rust and consume it? If Themistocles   65
Had lived obscured thus in th'Athenian state,
Xerxes had made both him and it his slaves.
If brave Camillus had lurked so in Rome,
He had not five times been Dictator there,
Nor four times triumphed. If Epaminondas,   70
Who lived twice twenty years obscured in Thebes,
Had lived so still, he had been still unnamed,
And paid his country nor himself their right;
But putting forth his strength, he rescued both
From imminent ruin, and like burnished steel,   75
After long use he shined; for as the light
Not only serves to show, but render us
Mutually profitable, so our lives
In acts exemplary not only win
Ourselves good names, but do to others give   80
Matter for virtuous deeds, by which we live.
    Bussy. What would you wish me do?
    Monsieur.   Leave the troubled streams,
And live, as thrivers do at the well-head.
    Bussy. At the well-head? Alas, what should I do
With that enchanted glass? See devils there?   85
Or, like a strumpet, learn to set my looks
In an eternal brake, or practise juggling,
To keep my face still fast, my heart still loose;
Or bear, like dame-school mistresses their riddles,
Two tongues, and be good only for a shift;   90
Flatter great lords, to put them still in mind
Why they were made lords; or please portly ladies
With a good carriage, tell them idle tales
To make their physic work; spend a man's life
In sights and visitations that will make   95
His eyes as hollow as his mistress' heart;
To do none good, but those that have no need;
To gain being forward, though you break for haste
All the commandments ere you break your fast,
But believe backwards, make your period   100

81 (see p. 79)   86–7 (see p. 79)   89 (see p. 80)
92 *portly* probably a low pun connected with 'carriage'
94 *physic* laxatives   100 (see p. 80)

And creed's last article, 'I believe in God';
And, hearing villainies preached, t'unfold their art
Learn to commit them? 'Tis a great man's part.
Shall I learn this there?
    Monsieur.   No, thou need'st not learn,
105 Thou hast the theory, now go there and practise.
    Bussy. Ay, in a threadbare suit; when men come there,
They must have high naps, and go from thence bare.
A man may drown the parts of ten rich men
In one poor suit; brave barks and outward gloss
110 Attract Court eyes, be in-parts ne'er so gross.
    Monsieur. Thou shalt have gloss enough, and all things
        fit
T'enchase in all show thy long-smothered spirit.
Be ruled by me then. The rude Scythians
Painted blind Fortune's powerful hands with wings
115 To show her gifts come swift and suddenly,
Which if her favourite be not swift to take,
He loses them for ever. Then be ruled;
Stay but awhile here and I'll send to thee.
        Exit MONSIEUR [*with the* PAGES]. BUSSY *remains*
    Bussy. What will he send? Some crowns? It is to sow
      them
120 Upon my spirit, and make them spring a crown
Worth millions of the seed-crowns he will send.
[Like to disparking noble husbandmen,
He'll put his plough into me, plough me up;
But his unsweating thrift is policy,
125 And learning-hating policy is ignorant
To fit his seed-land soil;] a smooth plain ground
Will never nourish any politic seed;
I am for honest actions, not for great:
If I may bring up a new fashion,
130 And rise in Court with virtue, speed his plough.
The King hath known me long as well as he,
Yet could my fortune never fit the length
Of both their understandings till this hour.
There is a deep nick in Time's restless wheel
135 For each man's good, when which nick comes, it strikes;

---

102 (see p. 80)   109 (see p. 80)
112 *T'enchase* set in gold   113 *rude* barbarous
122–6 (see p. 80)   122 (see p. 80)   124 (see p. 80)
134 *nick* reference to the striking mechanism of a clock

As rhetoric yet works not persuasion,
But only is a mean to make it work,
So no man riseth by his real merit,
But when it cries clink in his raiser's spirit.
Many will say, that cannot rise at all,   140
Man's first hour's rise is first step to his fall.
I'll venture that; men that fall low must die,
As well as men cast headlong from the sky.

Enter MAFFÉ.

Maffé.—Humour of princes! Is this man indued
With any merit worth a thousand crowns?   145
Will my lord have me be so ill a steward
Of his revenue, to dispose a sum
So great with so small cause as shows in him?
I must examine this.—Is your name D'Ambois?
   Bussy. Sir?
   Maffé.   Is your name D'Ambois?
   Bussy.   Who have we here?   150
Serve you the Monsieur?
   Maffé.   How?
   Bussy.   Serve you the Monsieur?
   Maffé. Sir, y'are very hot. I serve the Monsieur,
But in such place as gives me the command
Of all his other servants. And because
His Grace's pleasure is to give your good   155
A pass through my command, methinks you might
Use me with more good fashion.
   Bussy.   Cry you mercy.
Now you have opened my dull eyes, I see you,
And would be glad to see the good you speak of.
What might I call your name?
   Maffé.   Monsieur Maffé.   160
   Bussy. Monsieur Maffé? Then, good Monsieur Maffé,
Pray let me know you better.
   Maffé.   Pray do so,
That you may use me better. For yourself,
By your no better outside, I would judge you
To be a poet; have you given my lord   165
Some pamphlet?
   Bussy.   Pamphlet?
   Maffé.   Pamphlet, sir, I say.
   Bussy. Did his wise Excellency leave the good

142 *fall low* fall only from a low height   144 (see p. 81)

That is to pass your charge to my poor use
To your discretion?
    Maffé.   Though he did not, sir,
170 I hope 'tis no bad office to ask reason
How that his Grace gives me in charge, goes from me?
    Bussy. That's very perfect, sir.
    Maffé.   Why, very good, sir;
I pray, then, give me leave; if for no pamphlet,
May I not know what other merit in you
175 Makes his compunction willing to relieve you?
    Bussy. No merit in the world, sir.
    Maffé.   That is strange.
Y'are a poor soldier, are you?
    Bussy.   That I am, sir.
    Maffé. And have commanded?
    Bussy.   Ay, and gone without, sir.
    Maffé [aside] I see the man; a hundred crowns will make
      him
180 Swagger, and drink healths to his Highness' bounty,
And swear he could not be more bountiful.
So there's nine hundred crowns, saved.—Here, tall
      soldier,
His Grace hath sent you a whole hundred crowns.
    Bussy. A hundred, sir? Nay, do his Highness right;
185 I know his hand is larger, and perhaps
I may deserve more than my outside shows;
I am a scholar, as I am a soldier,
And I can poetise, and, being well encouraged,
May sing his fame for giving, yours for delivering
190 Like a most faithful steward what he gives.
    Maffé. What shall your subject be?
    Bussy.   I care not much
If to his Excellence I sing the praise
Of fair great noses, and to your deserts
The reverend virtues of a faithful steward.
195 What qualities have you, sir, beside your chain
And velvet jacket? Can your Worship dance?
    Maffé. [aside] A merry fellow, 'faith; it seems my lord
Will have him for his jester; and, believe it,
Such men are now no fools; 'tis a knight's place.
200 If I, to save my Lord some crowns, should urge him
T'abate his bounty, I should not be heard;

193 (see p.) 81
195-6 *chain and velvet jacket* symbols of a steward

I would to heaven I were an arrant ass,
For then I should be sure to have the ears
Of these great men, where now their jesters have them.
'Tis good to please him, yet I'll take no notice   205
Of his preferment, but in policy
Will still be grave and serious, lest he think
I fear his wooden dagger.—Here, Sir Ambo,
A thousand crowns I bring you from my lord;
Serve God, play the good husband; you may make   ·   210
This a good standing living: 'tis a bounty
His Highness might perhaps have bestowed better.
    Bussy. Go, y'are a rascal; hence, away, you rogue!
    Maffé. What mean you, sir?
    Bussy.   Hence! Prate no more,
Or, by thy villain's blood, thou prat'st thy last.   215
A barbarous groom grudge at his master's bounty!
But since I know he would as much abhor
His hind should argue what he gives his friend,
Take that, sir, for your aptness to dispute.
                        [Strikes him] Exit.
    Maffé. These crowns are sown in blood; blood be their /
        fruit.   220
                                      Exit.

Act I, Scene ii

HENRY, GUISE, MONTSURRY, ELENOR, TAMYRA, BEAUPRÉ,
    PERO, CHARLOTTE, PYRHA, ANNABLE.

    [HENRY *and* GUISE *are playing chess.*]

    Henry. Duchess of Guise, your Grace is much enriched
In the attendance of this English virgin
That will initiate her prime of youth,
Disposed to Court conditions, under hand
Of your preferred instructions and command,   5
Rather than any in the English Court,

208 (see p. 81)
210 *husband* connected with husbandry, good management
211 *good standing* settled, not casual or fluctuating
215 *villain* still carrying associations of 'villein', low-born
  2 *this English virgin* Annable

Whose ladies are not matched in Christendom
For graceful and confirmed behaviours,
More than the Court, where they are bred, is equalled.
10   *Guise.* I like not their Court form; it is too crestfallen
In all observance, making semi-gods
Of their great nobles, and of their old queen
An ever-young and most immortal goddess.
      Henry. Assure you, cousin Guise, so great a courtier,
15   So full of majesty and royal parts,
No queen in Christendom may boast herself.
Her Court approves it, that's a Court indeed,
Not mixt with rudeness used in common houses,
But, as Courts should be th'abstracts of their kingdoms
20   In all the beauty, state, and worth they hold,
So is hers, amply, and by her informed.
The world is not contracted in a man
With more proportion and expression
Than in her Court, her kingdom. Our French Court
25   Is a mere mirror of confusion to it:
The king and subject, lord and every slave,
Dance a continual hay; our rooms of state
Kept like our stables; no place more observed
Than a rude market-place: and though our custom
30   Keep this assured deformity from our sight,
'Tis ne'er the less essentially unsightly,
Which they would soon see, would they change their form
To this of ours, and then compare them both;
Which we must not affect, because in kingdoms
35   Where the king's change doth breed the subject's terror,
Pure innovation is more gross than error.
      Montsurry. No question we shall see them imitate,
Though afar off, the fashions of our Courts,
As they have ever aped us in attire;
40   Never were men so weary of their skins,
And apt to leap out of themselves as they,
Who, when they travel to bring forth rare men,
Come home delivered of a fine French suit;

---

8 *confirmed* firmly established in a system or according to a
convention
11 *observance* dutiful service, respect for rank   12 (see p. 81)
17 *approves* proves, demonstrates   19 *abstracts* epitomes
21 (see p. 81)   22 (see p. 81)
27 *hay* a winding country dance   34 *affect* aim at, desire
37–48 (see p. 81)   42 *travel* a pun on 'travail', labour

Their brains lie with their tailors, and get babies
For their most complete issue; he's first born   45
To all the moral virtues that first greets
The light with a new fashion, which becomes them
Like apes, disfigured with the attires of men.
    Henry. No question they much wrong their real worth
In affectation of outlandish scum;   50
But they have faults, and we; they foolish proud
To be the pictures of our vanity;
We proud that they are proud of foolery.

        Enter MONSIEUR [*and*] D'AMBOIS [*in fine clothes.*]

    Monsieur. Come, mine own sweetheart, I will enter thee
—Sir, I have brought this gentleman t'attend you,   55
And pray you would vouchsafe to do him grace.
    Henry. D'Ambois, I think.
    Bussy.   That's still my name, my lord,
Though I be something altered in attire.
    Henry. I like your alteration, and must tell you
I have expected th'offer of your service;   60
For we, in fear to make mild virtue proud,
Use not to seek her out in any man.
    Bussy. Nor doth she use to seek out any man:
He that will win, must woo her; she's not shameless.
    Monsieur. I urged her modesty in him, my lord,   65
And gave her those rites that he says she merits.
    Henry. If you have wooed and won, then, brother,
        wear him.
    Monsieur. Th'art mine, my love. See, here's the Guise's
Duchess, the Countess of Montsurry, Beaupré. Come, I'll
enseam thee. Ladies, y'are too many to be in Council; I   70
have here a friend that I would gladly enter in your graces.
    Duchess. If you enter him in our graces, methinks by his
blunt behaviour he should come out of himself.
    Tamyra. Has he never been courtier, my lord?
    Monsieur. Never, my lady.   75
    Beaupré. And why did the toy take him in th' head now?
    Bussy. 'Tis leap-year, lady, and therefore very good to
enter a courtier.
    Tamyra. The man's a courtier at first sight.

53 (see p. 81)   64 (see p. 81)
70 *enseam* introduce to company, usually with sexual implications
70 (see p. 81)   77 1604 was a leap-year

80   *Bussy.* I can sing prick-song, lady at first sight; and why not be a courtier as suddenly?

Beaupré. Here's a courtier rotten before he be ripe.

Bussy. Think me not impudent, lady; I am yet no courtier: I desire to be one, and would gladly take entrance,
85   madam, [*To the* DUCHESS] under your princely colours.

Enter BARRISOR, L'ANOU, PYRHOT.

Guise. Sir, know you me?

Bussy. My lord?

Guise. I know not you; whom do you serve?

Bussy. Serve, my lord!

90   *Guise.* Go to, companion, your courtship's too saucy.

Bussy. [*aside*] Saucy! Companion! 'Tis the Guise, but yet those terms might have been spared of the Guiserd. Companion! He's jealous, by this light. Are you blind of that side, sir. I'll to her again for that. Forth, Madam, for
95   the honour of courtship.

Guise. Cease your courtship, or by heaven I'll cut your throat.

Bussy. Cut my throat? Cut a whetstone! Good Accius Naevius, do as much with your tongue, as he did with a
100   razor: cut my throat!

Guise. I'll do't, by this hand.

Bussy. That hand dares not do't; y'ave cut too many throats already, Guise, and robbed the realm of many thousand souls more precious than thine own. Come,
105   Madam, talk on; 'sfoot, can you not talk? Talk on, I say; more courtship, as you love it.

Barrisor. What new-come gallant have we here that dares mate the Guise thus?

L'Anou. 'Sfoot, 'tis D'Ambois. The Duke mistakes him,
110   on my life, for some knight of the new edition.

Bussy. Cut my throat! I would the King feared thy cutting of his throat no more than I fear thy cutting of mine.

Guise. So, sir, so.

Pyrhot. Here's some strange distemper.

115   *Barrisor.* Here's a sudden transmigration with D'Ambois

---

80 (see p. 82)   82 (see p. 82)
90 *companion* fellow; used contemptuously (see also p. 86)
92 *Guiserd* Partisan of the Guise faction   98 (see p. 82)
102 (see p. 82)   108 *mate* checkmate, put out of countenance

—out of the knights' ward into the duchess' bed.

L'Anou. See what a metamorphosis a brave suit can work.

Pyrhot. 'Slight, step to the Guise and discover him.

Barrisor. By no means; let the new suit work; we'll see the issue.   120

Guise. Leave your courtship.

Bussy. I will not.—I say, mistress, and I will stand unto it, that if a woman may have three servants, a man may have threescore mistresses.

Guise. Sirrah, I'll have you whipped out of the Court for this insolence.   125

Bussy. Whipped? Such another syllable out o' th' presence, if thou darest for thy dukedom.

Guise. Remember, poltroon.

Monsieur.—Pray thee, forbear.   130

Bussy. Passion of death! Were not the King here, he should strow the chamber like a rush.

Monsieur. But leave courting his wife, then.

Bussy. I will not. I'll court her in despite of him. Not court her!—Come, madam, talk on, fear me nothing.—   135
[*To* GUISE] Well may'st thou drive thy master from the Court, but never D'Ambois.

Monsieur.—His great heart will not down, 'tis like the
          sea,
That partly by his own internal heat,
Partly the stars' daily and nightly motion,   140
Ardor and light, and partly of the place
The divers frames, and chiefly by the moon,
Bristled with surges, never will be won—
No, not when th' hearts of all those powers are burst—
To make retreat into his settled home,   145
Till he be crowned with his own quiet foam.

Henry. You have the mate. Another?

Guise. No more.

Exit GUISE; *after him the* KING, MONSIEUR *whispering.*

Barrisor. Why, here's the lion, scared with the throat of a dunghill cock; a fellow that has newly shaked off his   150
shackles; now does he crow for that victory.

---

116 (see p. 82)   118 *discover* reveal his identity
123 *servants* professed lovers
128 *th' presence* presence-chamber; the reception room of a palace
132 *like a rush* rushes were strewn on the floors of houses
142 (see p. 82)   147 (see p. 82)   149 (see p. 82)

L'Anou. 'Tis one of the best jigs that ever was acted.

Pyrhot. Whom does the Guise suppose him to be, trow?

L'Anou. Out of doubt, some new denizened lord, and
155   thinks that suit come new out o' th' mercer's books.

Barrisor. I have heard of a fellow, that by a fixed imagina-
tion looking upon a bull-baiting, had a visible pair of horns
grew out of his forehead, and I believe this gallant, over-
joyed with the conceit of Monsieur's cast suit, imagines
160   himself to be the Monsieur.

L'Anou. And why not? as well as the ass, stalking in the
lion's case, bare himself like a lion roaring all the huger
beasts out of the forest?

Pyrhot. Peace, he looks this way.

165   *Barrisor.* Marry, let him look, sir; what will you say now
if the Guise be gone to fetch a blanket for him?

L'Anou. Faith, I believe it for his honour.

Pyrhot. But, if D'Ambois carry it clean?

                                        Exeunt LADIES.

Barrisor. True, when he curvets in the blanket.

170   *Pyrhot.* Ay, marry, sir.

L'Anou. 'Sfoot, see how he stares on's.

Barrisor. Lord bless us, let's away.

Bussy. Now, sir, take your full view; how does the object
please ye?

175   *Barrisor.* If you ask my opinion, sir, I think your suit fits
as well as if't had been made for you.

Bussy. So, sir, and was that the subject of your ridiculous
jollity?

L'Anou. What's that to you, sir?

180   *Bussy.* Sir, I have observed all your fleerings, and resolve
yourselves ye shall give a strict account for't.

Enter BRISAC *and* MELYNELL.

Pyrhot. Oh, strange credulity! Do you think yourself such
a singular subject for laughter that none can fall into our
merriment but you?

185   *Barrisor.* This jealousy of yours, sir, confesses some close
defect in yourself that we never dreamed of.

L'Anou. We held discourse of a perfumed ass, that being

---

152 (see p. 82)   153 *trow* 'do you think?'
155 *mercer* dealer in silks and costly materials   159 *cast* cast off
161–2 (see p. 82)   162 *case* covering, skin
166 *blanket* to toss Bussy in
180 *fleerings* mocking looks and speeches   185 *close* hidden

disguised with a lion's case, imagined himself a lion: I hope
that touched not you.

Bussy. So, sir; your descants do marvellous well fit this   190
ground; we shall meet where your buffoonly laughters will
cost ye the best blood in your bodies.

Barrisor. For life's sake let's be gone; he'll kill's outright.

Bussy. Go at your pleasures, I'll be your ghost to haunt
you; and ye sleep on't, hang me.   195

L'Anou. Go, go, sir; court your mistress.

Pyrhot. And be advised; we shall have odds against you.

Bussy. Tush, valour stands not in number! I'll maintain
it that one man may beat three boys.

Brisac. Nay, you shall have no odds of him in number,   200
sir; he's a gentleman as good as the proudest of you, and
ye shall not wrong him.

Barrisor. Not, sir?

Melynell. Not, sir: though he be not so rich, he's a better
man than the best of you; and I will not endure it.   205

L'Anou. Not you, sir?

Brisac. No, sir, nor I.

Bussy. I should thank you for this kindness, if I thought
these perfumed musk-cats, being out of this privilege, durst
but once mew at us.   210

Barrisor. Does your confident spirit doubt that, sir?
Come follow us and try.

L'Anou. Come, sir, we'll lead you a dance.   *Exeunt.*

Act II, Scene i

HENRY, GUISE, BEAUMOND *and* ATTENDANTS.

Henry. This desperate quarrel sprung out of their envies
To D'Ambois' sudden bravery, and great spirit.

Guise. Neither is worth their envy.

Henry.   Less than either
Will make the gall of Envy overflow;
She feeds on outcast entrails like a kite;   5
In which foul heap, if any ill lies hid,
She sticks her beak into it, shakes it up,

190–1 (see p. 82)   209 *perfumed musk-cats* perfumed courtiers
209 (see p. 83)   s.d. (see p. 83)
  2 *bravery* courage; also, display, fine clothes

And hurls it all abroad, that all may view it.
Corruption is her nutriment; but touch her
10 With any precious ointment, and you kill her:
When she finds any filth in men, she feasts,
And with her black throat bruits it through the world
Being sound and healthful; but if she but taste
The slenderest pittance of commended virtue,
15 She surfeits of it, and is like a fly
That passes all the body's soundest parts,
And dwells upon the sores; or if her squint eye
Have power to find none there, she forges some.
She makes that crooked ever which is straight;
20 Calls valour giddiness, justice tyranny;
A wise man may shun her, she not herself:
Whithersoever she flies from her harms,
She bears her foe still clasped in her own arms;
And therefore, Cousin Guise, let us avoid her.

Enter NUNTIUS. *messenger*

25   *Nuntius.* What Atlas or Olympus lifts his head
So far past covert, that with air enough
My words may be informed, and from his height
I may be seen and heard through all the world?
A tale so worthy, and so fraught with wonder
30 Sticks in my jaws, and labours with event.
   Henry. Com'st thou from D'Ambois?
   Nuntius.   From him, and the rest,
His friends and enemies, whose stern fight I saw,
And heard their words before and in the fray.
   Henry. Relate at large what thou has seen and heard.
35   *Nuntius.* I saw fierce D'Ambois and his two brave friends
Enter the field, and at their heels their foes;
Which were the famous soldiers, Barrisor,
L'Anou, and Pyrhot, great in deeds of arms:
All which arrived at the evenest piece of earth
40 The field afforded, the three challengers
Turned head, drew all their rapiers, and stood ranked,
When face to face the three defendants met them,
Alike prepared, and resolute alike,

12 *bruits* noises abroad
13 *Being sound and healthful* i.e. as being, referring to 'filth' 24
   s.d. (see p. 83)
26 *covert* covering, of trees, etc.   27 *informed* given form
30 *event* outcome, a coming to birth   35 (see p. 83)
39–47 (see p. 83)

Like bonfires of contributory wood:
Every man's look shewed, fed with either's spirit,   45
As one had been a mirror to another,
Like forms of life and death; each took from other;
And so were life and death mixed at their heights,
That you could see no fear of death, for life,
Nor love of life, for death; but in their brows   50
Pyrrho's opinion in great letters shone,
That life and death in all respects are one.
    Henry. Passed there no sort of words at their encounter?
    Nuntius. As Hector, 'twixt the hosts of Greece and Troy,
When Paris and the Spartan king should end   55
The nine years' war, held up his brazen lance
For signal that both hosts should cease from arms
And hear him speak; so Barrisor, advised,
Advanced his naked rapier 'twixt both sides,
Ripped up the quarrel, and compared six lives   60
Then laid in balance with six idle words;
Offered remission and contrition too;
Or else that he and D'Ambois might conclude
The others' dangers. D'Ambois liked the last;
But Barrisor's friends, being equally engaged   65
In the main quarrel, never would expose
His life alone to that they all deserved.   *biased?*
And—for the other offer of remission—
D'Ambois, that like a laurel put in fire
Sparkled and spit, did much much more than scorn   70
That his wrong should incense him so like chaff
To go so soon out, and like lighted paper
Approve his spirit at once both fire and ashes;
So drew they lots, and in them Fates appointed
That Barrisor should fight with fiery D'Ambois,   75
Pyrhot with Melynell, with Brisac, L'Anou:
And then like flame and powder they commixed
So spritely that I wished they had been spirits,
That the ne'er-shutting wounds they needs must open
Might, as they opened, shut and never kill: 80
But D'Ambois' sword, that lightened as it flew,
Shot like a pointed comet at the face

44 (see p. 83)
51 *Pyrrho* Greek sceptic of the time of Alexander the Great
54 (see p. 83)   58 *advised* having deliberated
60 (see p. 83)   63 (see p. 83)   78 *spritely* spiritedly
78–80 (see p. 84)

Of manly Barrisor, and there it stuck:
Thrice plucked he at it, and thrice drew on thrusts
85 From him that of himself was free as fire;
Who thrust still as he plucked, yet (past belief!)
He with his subtle eye, hand, body, scaped;
At last, the deadly-bitten point tugged off,
On fell his yet undaunted foe so fiercely
90 That, only made more horrid with his wound,
Great D'Ambois shrunk, and gave a little ground;
But soon returned, redoubled in his danger,
And at the heart of Barrisor sealed his anger:
Then, as in Arden I have seen an oak
95 Long shook with tempests, and his lofty top
Bent to his root, which being at length made loose,
Even groaning with his weight, he gan to nod
This way and that, as loath his curled brows,
Which he had oft wrapt in the sky with storms,
100 Should stoop; and yet, his radical fibres burst,
Storm-like he fell, and hid the fear-cold earth:
So fell stout Barrisor, that had stood the shocks
Of ten set battles in your Highness' war
Gainst the sole soldier of the world, Navarre.
　　Guise. Oh, piteous and horrid murther!
105 　　*Beaumond.* 　　　　　　　　　　Such a life
Methinks had metal in it to survive
An age of men.
　　Henry. 　　　　Such often soonest end.
—Thy felt report calls on; we long to know
On what events the other have arrived.
110 　　*Nuntius.* Sorrow and fury, like two opposite fumes
Met in the upper region of a cloud,
At the report made by this worthy's fall
Brake from the earth, and with them rose Revenge,
Entering with fresh powers his two noble friends;
115 And under that odds fell surcharged Brisac,
The friend of D'Ambois, before fierce L'Anou;
Which D'Ambois seeing, as I once did see,
In my young travels through Armenia,

84–7 (see p. 84)　　　　　89 (see p. 84)
92 *redoubled* a fencing term; to repeat a blow
93 *sealed* impressed, as with a seal; (Brooke), hence, finished off
94 (see p. 84)　　　　104 (see p. 84)　　　　108 (see p. 84)
110 (see p. 84)　　　　115 *surcharged* overloaded, weighed down
118 (see p. 84)

An angry unicorn in his full career
Charge with too quick an eye a jeweller,   120
That watched him for the treasure of his brow,
And ere he could get shelter of a tree,
Nail him with his rich antler to the earth:
So D'Ambois ran upon revenged L'Anou,
Who eyeing th' eager point borne in his face,   125
And giving back, fell back, and in his fall
His foes uncurbed sword stopped in his heart:
By which time all the life-strings of the tw'other
Were cut, and both fell as their spirits flew
Upwards, and still hunt honour at the view.   130
And now, of all the six, sole D'Ambois stood
Untouched, save only with the others' blood.
    Henry. All slain outright?
    Nuntius.   All slain outright but he,
Who kneeling in the warm life of his friends,
All freckled with the blood his rapier rained,   135
He kissed their pale cheeks, and bade both farewell;
And see the bravest man the French earth bears.   *but bloodthirsty*

        Enter MONSIEUR, [*and*] D'AMBOIS *bare.*

    Bussy. Now is the time; y'are princely vowed, my friend;
Perform it princely, and obtain my pardon.
    Monsieur. Else heaven forgive not me; come on, brave   140
friend.   [*They kneel before* HENRY.]
If ever Nature held herself her own,
When the great trial of a king and subject
Met in one blood, both from one belly springing,
Now prove her virtue and her greatness one,
Or make the t'one the greater with the t'other,   145
As true kings should, and for your brother's love,
Which is a special species of true virtue,
Do that you could not do, not being a king.
    Henry. Brother, I know your suit; these wilful murthers
Are ever past our pardon.
    Monsieur.   Manly slaughter   150
Should never bear th'account of wilful murther;
It being a spice of justice, where with life
Offending past law equal life is laid
In equal balance, to scourge that offence
By law of reputation, which to men   155

119–23 (see p. 84)   130 (see p. 84)   135 (see p. 84)
137 s.d. *bare* bare-headed   141–8 (see p. 84–5)   150–9 (see p. 85)

Exceeds all positive law, and what that leaves
To true men's valours, not prefixing rights
Of satisfaction suited to their wrongs,
A free man's eminence may supply and take.

    Henry. This would make every man that thinks him
160   wronged
Or is offended, or in wrong or right,
Lay on this violence; and all vaunt themselves
Law-menders and suppliers, though mere butchers,
Should this fact, though of justice, be forgiven.

165   *Monsieur.* Oh, no, my lord; it would make cowards fear
To touch the reputations of full men;
When only they are left to imp the law,
Justice will soon distinguish murtherous minds
From just revengers: had my friend been slain,
170 His enemy surviving, he should die,
Since he had added to a murthered fame,
Which was in his intent, a murthered man;
And this had worthily been wilful murther;
But my friend only saved his fame's dear life,
175 Which is above life, taking th'under value,
Which, in the wrong it did, was forfeit to him;
And in this fact only preserves a man
In his uprightness, worthy to survive
Millions of such as murther men alive.

180   *Henry.* Well, brother, rise, and raise your friend withal
From death to life; and, D'Ambois, let your life,
Refined by passing through this merited death,
Be purged from more such foul pollution;
Nor on your scape, nor valour, more presuming
To be again so violent.

185   *Bussy.*   My lord,
I loathe as much a deed of unjust death,
As law itself doth; and to tyrannize,
Because I have a little spirit to dare
And power to do, as to be tyrannized.
190 This is a grace that, on my knees redoubled,
I crave to double this my short life's gift,

163–4 (see p. 85)   166 (see p. 85)
167 *imp* add to, supply the defects of
170 *he should die* i.e. his enemy
175 (see p. 85)   179 (see p. 85)   180 *withal* as well
184 *scape* escape
190 *redoubled* kneeling a second time (see also p. 85)

And shall your royal bounty centuple,
That I may so make good what God and Nature
Have given me for my good: since I am free,
Offending no just law, let no law make   195
By any wrong it does, my life her slave:
When I am wronged, and that law fails to right me,
Let me be king myself, as man was made,
And do a justice that exceeds the law;
If my wrong pass the power of single valour   200
To right and expiate, then be you my king,
And do a right, exceeding Law and Nature:
Who to himself is law, no law doth need,
Offends no king, and is a king indeed.
    Henry. Enjoy what thou entreatest; we give but ours.   205
    Bussy. What you have given, my lord, is ever yours.
               Exit KING, BEAUMOND, *and* ATTENDANTS
    Guise. Mort Dieu, who would have pardoned such a
        murther?   *Exit*
    Monsieur. Now vanish horrors into Court attractions,
For which let this balm make thee fresh and fair.
    Bussy. How shall I quite your love?
    Monsieur.   Be true to the end: 210
I have obtained a kingdom with my friend.   *Exeunt*

Act II, Scene ii

[*Enter*] MONTSURRY, TAMYRA, BEAUPRÉ, PERO [*with a book*]
             CHARLOTTE, PYRHA.

    Montsurry. He will have pardon sure.
    Tamyra.   'Twere pity else;
For though his great spirit something overflow,
All faults are still borne that from greatness grow.
But such a sudden courtier saw I never.
    Beaupré. He was too sudden, which indeed was rudeness.   5
    Tamyra. True, for it argued his no due conceit
Both of the place and greatness of the persons,
Nor of our sex; all which—we all being strangers

192 *And shall* a grace which shall . . .' (Boas)   (See also p. 85)
210 *quite* requite   211 (see p. 85)
  3 (see p. 86)   6 *conceit* opinion, esteem

To his encounter—should have made more manners
Deserve more welcome.
10   *Montsurry.*   All this fault is found
Because he loved the Duchess and left you.
    Tamyra. Alas, love give her joy. I am so far
From envy of her honour that I swear,
Had he encountered me with such proud sleight,
15 I would have put that project face of his
To a more test than did her Duchess-ship.
    Beaupré. Why, by your leave, my lord, I'll speak it here,
Although she be my aunt, she scarce was modest,
When she perceived the Duke her husband take
20 Those late exceptions to her servant's courtship,
To entertain him.
    Tamyra. Aye and stand him still,
Letting her husband give her servant place.
Though he did manly, she should be a woman.
                    Enter GUISE.
    Guise. D'Ambois is pardoned! Where's a king? Where
law?
25 See how it runs, much like a turbulent sea;
Here high and glorious, as it did contend
To wash the heavens and make the stars more pure;
And here so low, it leaves the mud of hell
To every common view. Come, Count Montsurry,
We must consult of this.
30   *Tamyra.*   Stay not, sweet lord.
    Montsurry. Be pleased, I'll straight return.
                              Exit with GUISE.
    Tamyra.   Would that would please me.
    Beaupré. I'll leave you, Madam, to your passions.
I see there's change of weather in your looks.
[*Exit with* CHARLOTTE *and* PYRHA. PERO *remains reading her*
                    book.]
    Tamyra. I cannot cloak it; but as when a fume,
35 Hot, dry and gross, within the womb of earth
Or in her superficies begot,
When extreme cold hath struck it to her heart,
The more it is compressed, the more it rageth,
Exceeds his prison's strength that should contain it,

---

9 *encounter* accosting, making advances to someone
14 *sleight* stratagem   15 (see p. 86)
25 *See how it runs* i.e. the law   34 (see p. 86)
36 *superficies* surface, outside

And then it tosseth temples in the air,   40
All bars made engines to his insolent fury;
So, of a sudden, my licentious fancy
Riots within me. Not my name and house
Nor my religion to this hour observed
Can stand above it; I must utter that   45
That will in parting break more strings in me
Than death when life parts; and that holy man
That, from my cradle, counselled for my soul,
I now must make an agent for my blood.

Enter MONSIEUR.

Monsieur. Yet is my mistress gracious?
Tamyra.   Yet unanswered?   50
Monsieur. Pray thee regard thine own good, if not mine,
And cheer my love for that; you do not know
What you may be by me, nor what without me;
I may have power t'advance and pull down any.
Tamyra. That's not my study; one way I am sure   55
You shall not pull down me; my husband's height
Is crown to all my hopes; and his retiring
To any mean state shall be my aspiring:
Mine honour's in mine own hands, spite of kings.
Monsieur. Honour, what's that? Your second maiden-
    head: 60
And what is that? A word: the word is gone,
The thing remains: the rose is plucked, the stalk
Abides; an easy loss where no lack's found:
Believe it, there's as small lack in the loss
As there is pain i'th' losing; archers ever   65
Have two strings to a bow; and shall great Cupid,
Archer of archers both in men and women,
Be worse provided than a common archer?
A husband and a friend all wise wives have.
Tamyra. Wise wives they are that on such strings depend, 70
With a firm husband weighing a dissolute friend.
Monsieur. Still you stand on your husband; so do all
The common sex of you, when y'are encountered
With one ye cannot fancy: all men know
You live in Court here by your own election,   75
Frequenting all our solemn sports and triumphs,
All the most youthful company of men:
And wherefore do you this? To please your husband?

41 (see p. 86)   49 (see p. 86)   51 (see p. 86)

'Tis gross and fulsome: if your husband's pleasure
80 Be all your object, and you aim at honour,
In living close to him, get you from Court;
You may have him at home; these common put-offs
For common women serve: 'My honour! Husband!'
Dames maritorious ne'er were meritorious:
85 Speak plain, and say 'I do not like you, sir;
Y'are an ill-favoured fellow in my eye',
And I am answered.
    Tamyra.   Then, I pray, be answered:
For, in good faith, my lord, I do not like you
In that sort you like.
    Monsieur.   Then have at you here!
90 Take with a politic hand this rope of pearl,
And though you be not amorous, yet be wise:
Take me for wisdom; he that you can love
Is ne'er the further from you.
    Tamyra.   Now it comes
So ill prepared, that I may take a poison
95 Under a medicine as good cheap as it;
I will not have it were it worth the world.
    Monsieur. Horror of death! Could I but please your eye,
You would give me the like, ere you would loose me.
'Honour and husband!'
    Tamyra.   By this light, my lord,
100 Y'are a vile fellow, and I'll tell the King
Your occupation of dishonouring ladies,
And of his Court: a lady cannot live
As she was born, and with that sort of pleasure
That fits her state, but she must be defamed
105 With an infamous lord's detraction.
Who would endure the Court if these attempts
Of open and professed lust must be borne?—
Who's there? [*To* PERO] Come on, dame, you are at your book
When men are at your mistress; have I taught you
110 Any such waiting-woman's quality?
    Monsieur. Farewell, 'good husband!'
                      Exit MONSIEUR.
    Tamyra.   Farewell, wicked lord!

Enter MONTSURRY.

81 *living close* privately, shut away from all others
84 (see p. 86)   94–5 (see p. 86)

Montsurry. Was not the Monsieur here?
Tamyra.   Yes, to good purpose;
And your cause is as good to seek him too,
And haunt his company.
Montsurry.   Why, what's the matter?
Tamyra. Matter of death, were I some husband's wife;   115
I cannot live at quiet in my chamber
For opportunities almost to rapes
Offered me by him.
Montsurry.   Pray thee bear with him:
Thou know'st he is a bachelor and a courtier,
Ay, and a prince; and their prerogatives   120
Are to their laws, as to their pardons are
Their reservations, after Parliaments—
One quits another: form gives all their essence:
That prince doth high in virtue's reckoning stand
That will entreat a vice, and not command: 125
So far bear with him; should another man
Trust to his privilege, he should trust to death.
Take comfort, then, my comfort, nay, triumph
And crown thyself; thou partest with victory:
My presence is so only dear to thee   130
That other men's appear worse than they be.
For this night yet, bear with my forced absence;
Thou knowest my business, and with how much weight
My vow hath charged it.
Tamyra.   True, my lord, and never
My fruitless love shall let your serious profit;   135
Yet, sweet lord, do not stay; you know my soul
Is so long time without me, and I dead
As you are absent.
Montsurry.   By this kiss, receive
My soul for hostage, till I see my love.
Tamyra. The morn shall let me see you?
Montsurry.   With the sun   140
I'll visit thy more comfortable beauties.
Tamyra. This is my comfort, that the sun hath left
The whole world's beauty ere my sun leaves me.
Montsurry. 'Tis late night now, indeed; farewell, my
      light.   *Exit.*

---

115 (see p. 86)   117 *opportunities* importunities
120–3 (see p. 86–7)   129 *partest* depart, come off victoriously
134 *charged* loaded   135 *let* hinder
136 *stay* remain away   136–43 (see p. 87)
137 *without* outside of, away from

145   *Tamyra.* Farewell, my light and life. But not in him,
      [In mine own dark love and light bent to another.]
      Alas, that in the wane of our affections
      We should supply it with a full dissembling,
      In which each youngest maid is grown a mother.
150   Frailty is fruitful, one sin gets another:
      Our loves like sparkles are, that brightest shine
      When they go out; most vice shows most divine.
      —Go, maid, to bed; lend me your book, I pray:
      Not, like yourself, for form; I'll this night trouble
155   None of your services: make sure the doors,
      And call your other fellows to their rest.
          Pero. [*aside*] I will.—Yet I will watch to know why you
                watch.   *Exit.*
          Tamyra. Now all the peaceful regents of the night,
      Silently-gliding exhalations,
160   Languishing winds, and murmuring falls of waters,
      Sadness of heart and ominous secureness,
      Enchantments, dead sleeps, all the friends of rest,
      That ever wrought upon the life of man,
      Extend your utmost strengths, and this charmed hour
165   Fix like the Centre! Make the violent wheels
      Of Time and Fortune stand, and great Existence,
      The Maker's treasury, now not seem to be,
      To all but my approaching friends and me!
      They come, alas, they come! Fear, fear and hope
170   Of one thing, at one instant, fight in me:
      I love what most I loathe, and cannot live,
      Unless I compass that which holds my death:
      For love is hateful without love again,
      And he I love, will loathe me, when he sees
175   I fly my sex, my virtue, my renown,
      To run so madly on a man unknown.   *The vault opens.*
      See, see, the gulf is opening that will swallow
      Me and my fame for ever; I will in,
      And cast myself off, as I ne'er had been.

                                                          Exit.

                FRIAR *and* D'AMBOIS *ascend.*

180   *Friar.* Come, worthiest son, I am past measure glad

      146 (see p. 87)
      147 *wane* A and B, 'wave'. The emendation is Dilke's
      147–49 (see p. 87)   151 *sparkles* sparks   152 (see p. 87)
      158 *regents* rulers   161 (see p. 87)   165 (see p. 87)
      165–6 (see p. 87)   167 (see p. 87)   179 (see p. 87–8)

That you, whose worth I have approved so long,
Should be the object of her fearful love;
Since both your wit and spirit can adapt
Their full force to supply her utmost weakness.
You know her worths and virtues, for report   185
Of all that know is to a man a knowledge:
You know, besides, that our affections' storm,
Raised in our blood, no reason can reform.
Though she seek then their satisfaction,
Which she must needs, or rest unsatisfied,   190
Your judgment will esteem her peace thus wrought
Nothing less dear than if yourself had sought:
And with another colour, which my art
Shall teach you to lay on, yourself must seem
The only agent, and the first orb move   195
In this our set and cunning world of love.
    Bussy. Give me the colour, my most honoured father,
And trust my cunning then to lay it on.
    Friar. 'Tis this, good son; Lord Barrisor, whom you
        slew,
Did love her dearly, and with all fit means   200
Hath urged his acceptation, of all which
She keeps one letter written in his blood.
You must say thus, then, that you heard from me
How much herself was touched in conscience
With a report—which is, in truth, dispersed—   205
That your main quarrel grew about her love,
Lord Barrisor imagining your courtship
Of the great Guise's Duchess, in the Presence,
Was by you made to his elected mistress;
And so made me your mean now to resolve her   210
Choosing by my direction this night's depth
For the more clear avoiding of all note
Of your presumed presence; and with this,
To clear her hands of such a lover's blood,
She will so kindly thank and entertain you,   215
Methinks I see how—ay, and ten to one,
Show you the confirmation in his blood,
Lest you should think report and she did feign,

181 *approved* made proof of   193 (see p. 88)
195 (see p. 88)   196 (see p. 88)   199 (see p. 88)
205 *dispersed* spread abroad   210 *resolve* explain the truth
213 *presumed* presumptuous
217 *the confirmation* i.e. the letter written in his blood

That you shall so have circumstantial means
220 To come to the direct, which must be used;
For the direct is crooked; love comes flying;
The height of love is still won with denying.
    Bussy. Thanks, honour'd father.
    Friar.   She must never know
That you know anything of any love
225 Sustained on her part; for, learn this of me,
In anything a woman does alone,
If she dissemble, she thinks 'tis not done;
If not dissemble, nor a little chide,
Give her her wish, she is not satisfied;
230 To have a man think that she never seeks
Does her more good than to have all she likes:
This frailty sticks in them beyond their sex,
Which to reform, reason is too perplex:
Urge reason to them, it will do no good;
235 Humour, that is the chariot of our food
In everybody, must in them be fed,
To carry their affections by it bred.
Stand close!

             Enter TAMYRA *with a book.*

    Tamyra. Alas, I fear my strangeness will retire him.
240 If he go back, I die; I must prevent it,
And cheer his onset with my sight at least,
And that's the most; though every step he takes
Goes to my heart, I'll rather die than seem
Not to be strange to that I most esteem.
    Friar. Madam!
    Tamyra.   Ah!
245   *Friar.*   You will pardon me, I hope,
That so beyond your expectation
And at a time for visitants so unfit
I, with my noble friend here, visit you.
You know that my access at any time
250 Hath ever been admitted; and that friend
That my care will presume to bring with me
Shall have all circumstance of worth in him
To merit as free welcome as myself.

---

219 *circumstantial* round about   228–9 (see p. 88)
233 *perplex* perplexed, puzzled   235–7 (see p. 88)
239 *strangeness* coldness

Tamyra. Oh, father, but at this suspicious hour
You know how apt best men are to suspect us   255
In any cause that makes suspicious shadow
No greater than the shadow of a hair:
And y'are to blame. What though my lord and husband
Lie forth to-night, and since I cannot sleep
When he is absent I sit up to-night;   260
Though all the doors are sure, and all our servants
As sure bound with their sleeps; yet there is One
That sits above, whose eye no sleep can bind;
He sees through doors, and darkness, and our thoughts;
And therefore as we should avoid with fear   265
To think amiss ourselves before his search,
So should we be as curious to shun
All cause that other think not ill of us.
  Bussy. Madam, 'tis far from that; I only heard
By this my honoured father that your conscience   270
Was something troubled with a false report
That Barrisor's blood should something touch your hand,
Since he imagined I was courting you,
When I was bold to change words with the Duchess,
And therefore made his quarrel, which my presence,   275
Presumed on with my father at this season
For the more care of your so curious honour,
Can well resolve your conscience is most false.
  Tamyra. And is it therefore that you come, good sir?
Then crave I now your pardon and my father's,   280
And swear your presence does me so much comfort,
That all I have it binds to your requital:
Indeed, sir, 'tis most true that a report
Is spread, alleging that his love to me
Was reason of your quarrel; and because   285
You shall not think I feign it for my glory
That he importuned me for his court service,
I'll show you his own hand, set down in blood,
To that vain purpose: good sir, then come in.
Father, I thank you now a thousandfold.   290
                    Exit TAMYRA *and* D'AMBOIS.
  Friar. May it be worth it to you, honoured daughter.
                              The FRIAR *descends.*

264 (see p. 88)   267 *curious* careful
276 *Presumed on with* presumptuously arranged with the help of
287 *court service* fashionable philandering (McIlwraith)

Act III, Scene i

Enter D'AMBOIS, TAMYRA.

    Tamyra. Oh my dear servant, in thy close embraces
I have set open all the doors of danger
To my encompassed honour, and my life.
Before I was secure against death and hell;
5   But now am subject to the heartless fear
Of every shadow, and of every breath,
And would change firmness with an aspen leaf:
So confident a spotless conscience is,
So weak a guilty: oh, the dangerous siege
10   Sin lays about us, and the tyranny
He exercises when he hath expugned!
Like to the horror of a winter's thunder,
Mix'd with a gushing storm, that suffer nothing
To stir abroad on earth but their own rages,
15   Is Sin, when it hath gathered head above us:
No roof, no shelter can secure us so,
But he will drown our cheeks in fear or woe.
    Bussy. Sin is a coward, madam, and insults
But on our weakness, in his truest valour,
20   And so our ignorance tames us, that we let
His shadows fright us; and like empty clouds,
In which our faulty apprehensions forge
The forms of dragons, lions, elephants,
When they hold no proportion, the sly charms
25   Of the witch Policy makes him like a monster
Kept only to show men for goddess money:
That false hag often paints him in her cloth
Ten times more monstrous than he is in troth.
In three of us the secret of our meeting
30   Is only guarded, and three friends as one
Have ever been esteemed, as our three powers
That in our one soul are as one united:
Why should we fear then? For my truth, I swear,

---

3 *encompassed* surrounded   5 *heartless* spiritless
9–28 (see p. 88)   11 *expugned* taken by storm
18 *insults* triumphs only over
19 *in his truest valour* even when he is most valorous
22 *apprehensions* understandings
24 (see p. 88)   25–7 (see p. 88)   31–2 (see pp. 88–9)

Sooner shall torture be the sire to pleasure,
And health be grievous to men long time sick,   35
Than the dear jewel of your fame in me
Be made an outcast to your infamy;
Nor shall my value, sacred to your virtues,
Only give free course to it from myself,
But make it fly out of the mouths of kings   40
In golden vapours and with awful wings.
   Tamyra. It rests as all kings' seals were set in thee.
                     Exit D'AMBOIS. TAMYRA *remains.*
It is not I, but urgent destiny.
That—as great statesmen for their general end
In politic justice, make poor men offend—   45
Enforceth my offence to make it just.
What shall weak dames do, when th' whole work of nature
Hath a strong finger in each one of us?
Needs must that sweep away the silly cobweb
Of our still-undone labours: that lays still   50
Our powers to it, as to the line the stone,
Not to the stone the line should be opposed.
We cannot keep our constant course in virtue:
What is alike at all parts? Every day
Differs from other, every hour and minute;   55
Ay, every thought in our false clock of life
Oft-times inverts the whole circumference:
We must be sometimes one, sometimes another.
Our bodies are but thick clouds to our souls,
Through which they cannot shine when they desire.   60
When all the stars, and even the sun himself,
Must stay the vapours' times that he exhales
Before he can make good his beams to us,
Oh, how can we, that are but motes to him,
Wandering at random in his ordered rays,   65
Disperse our passions' fumes, with our weak labours,
That are more thick and black than all earth's vapours?

                Enter MONTSURRY.

   Montsurry. Good day, my love! What, up and ready too!
   Tamyra. Both, my dear lord; not all this night made I
Myself unready, or could sleep a wink.   70

38 *value* valour and worth   42 (see p. 89)
44–6 (see p. 89)   50 (see p. 89)   50–2 (see p. 89)
52 *opposed* aligned   57 (see p. 89)   61 (see p. 89)
62 *stay* await   62 *exhales* draws up   70 *unready* undressed

Montsurry. Alas, what troubled my true love, my peace,
From being at peace within her better self?
Or how could sleep forbear to seize thy beauties
When he might challenge them as his just prize?

75   *Tamyra.* I am in no power earthly, but in yours;
To what end should I go to bed, my lord,
That wholly missed the comfort of my bed?
Or how should sleep possess my faculties,
Wanting the proper closer of mine eyes?

80   *Montsurry.* Then will I never more sleep night from thee:
All mine own business, all the King's affairs,
Shall take the day to serve them; every night
I'll ever dedicate to thy delight.
    Tamyra. Nay, good my lord, esteem not my desires

85   Such doters on their humours that my judgment
Cannot subdue them to your worthier pleasure:
A wife's pleased husband must her object be
In all her acts, not her soothed fantasy.
    Montsurry. Then come, my love, now pay those rites to sleep

90   Thy fair eyes owe him; shall we now to bed?
    Tamyra. Oh, no, my lord; your holy friar says
All couplings in the day that touch the bed
Adulterous are, even in the married;
Whose grave and worthy doctrine, well I know,

95   Your faith in him will liberally allow.
    Montsurry. He's a most learned and religious man;
Come to the presence then, and see great D'Ambois,
Fortune's proud mushroom shot up in a night,
Stand like an Atlas underneath the King;

100   Which greatness with him Monsieur now envies
As bitterly and deadly as the Guise.
    Tamyra. What! He that was but yesterday his maker,
His raiser, and preserver?
    Montsurry.   Even the same.
Each natural agent works but to this end,

105   To render that it works on like itself;
Which since the Monsieur in his act on D'Ambois
Cannot to his ambitious end effect,
But that, quite opposite, the King hath power,
In his love borne to D'Ambois, to convert

110   The point of Monsieur's aim on his own breast,

---

85 *humours* whims   88 *fantasy* caprice, desire
98 (see p. 89)   99 (see p. 89)

He turns his outward love to inward hate:
A prince's love is like the lightning's fume,
Which no man can embrace but must consume.

Exeunt.

Act III, Scene ii

HENRY, D'AMBOIS, MONSIEUR, GUISE, DUCHESS,
ANNABLE, CHARLOTTE, ATTENDANTS.

a favourite of the King

Henry. Speak home, my Bussy! Thy impartial words
Are like brave falcons that dare truss a fowl
Much greater than themselves; flatterers are kites
That check at nothing; thou shalt be my eagle,
And bear my thunder underneath thy wings;   5
Truth's words, like jewels, hang in th' ears of kings.
Bussy. Would I might live to see no Jews hang there
Instead of jewels—sycophants, I mean,
Who use Truth like the Devil, his true foe,
Cast by the angel to the pit of fears,   10
And bound in chains; Truth seldom decks kings' ears.
Slave Flattery, like a rippier's legs rolled up
In boots of hay-ropes, with kings' soothed guts
Swaddled and strappled, now lives only free.
Oh, 'tis a subtle knave; how like the plague   15
Unfelt he strikes into the brain of truth,
And rageth in his entrails when he can,
Worse than the poison of a red-haired man.
Henry. Fly at him and his brood! I cast thee off,
And once more give thee surname of mine eagle.   20
Bussy. I'll make you sport enough, then: let me have
My lucerns too, or dogs inured to hunt
Beasts of most rapine, but to put them up,
And if I truss not, let me not be trusted.
Show me a great man by the people's voice,   25
Which is the voice of God, that by his greatness
Bombasts his private roofs with public riches;

2 *truss* seize a prey in its talons   4 (see p. 89)
5 (see pp. 89–90)   9–14 (see p. 90)   12 *rippier* seller of fish
13 *soothed* flattered (see also p. 90)
14 *strappled* furnished with coverings for the legs
18 (see p. 90)   22 *inured* trained (see also p. 90)
27 *Bombasts* stuffs out

That affects royalty, rising from a clapdish;
That rules so much more than his suffering king,
30   That he makes kings of his subordinate slaves:
Himself and them graduate—like woodmongers,
Piling a stack of billets—from the earth,
Raising each other into steeples' heights;
Let him convey this on the turning props
35   Of Protean law, and, his own counsel keeping,
Keep all upright—let me but hawk at him,
I'll play the vulture, and so thump his liver,
That, like a huge unlading Argosy,
He shall confess all, and you then may hang him.
40   Show me a clergyman, that is in voice
A lark of heaven, in heart a mole of earth;
That hath good living, and a wicked life;
A temperate look, and a luxurious gut;
Turning the rents of his superfluous cures
45   Into your pheasants and your partridges,
Venting their quintessence as men read Hebrew—
Let me but hawk at him, and, like the other,
He shall confess all, and you then may hang him.
Show me a lawyer that turns sacred law—
50   The equal renderer of each man his own,
The scourge of rapine and extortion,
The sanctuary and impregnable defence
Of retired learning and oppressed virtue—
Into a harpy, that eats all but 's own,
55   Into the damned sins it punisheth,
Into the synagogue of thieves and atheists,
Blood into gold, and justice into lust—
Let me but hawk at him, as at the t'other,
He shall confess all, and you then may hang him.

Enter MONTSURRY, TAMYRA, *and* PERO.

Guise. Where will you find such game as you would
60   hawk at?
Bussy. I'll hawk about your house for one of them.
Guise. Come, y'are a glorious ruffian, and run proud

28 *affects* assumes ostentatiously; *clapdish* beggar's bowl
29 (see p. 90)   31–6 (see p. 90)   35 (see p. 90)
37 (see p. 91)   38 *unlading* unloading   44 (see p. 91)
46 *as men read Hebrew* i.e. backwards, at the back end
50 *equal* impartial
62 *glorious* boastful; *run proud* to be on heat, as well as normal
    meaning

Of the King's headlong graces; hold your breath,
Or, by that poison'd vapour, not the King
Shall back your murtherous valour against me.   65
    Bussy. I would the King would make his presence free
But for one charge betwixt us: by the reverence
Due to the sacred space 'twixt kings and subjects,
Here would I make thee cast that popular purple,
In which thy proud soul sits and braves thy sovereign.   70
    Monsieur. Peace, peace, I pray thee peace.
    Bussy.   Let him peace first
That made the first war.
    Monsieur.   He's the better man.
    Bussy. And, therefore, may do worst?
    Monsieur.   He has more titles.
    Bussy. So Hydra had more heads.
    Monsieur.   He's greater known.
    Bussy. His greatness is the people's; mine's mine own.   75
    Monsieur. He's nobly born.
    Bussy.   He is not; I am noble.
And noblesse in his blood hath no gradation,
But in his merit.
    Guise.   Th'art not nobly born,
But bastard to the Cardinal of Ambois.
    Bussy. Thou liest, proud Guisard; let me fly, my lord.   80
    Henry. Not in my face, my eagle; violence flies
The sanctuaries of a prince's eyes.
    Bussy. Still shall we chide and foam upon this bit?
Is the Guise only great in faction?
Stands he not by himself? Proves he th' opinion   85
That men's souls are without them? Be a duke,
And lead me to the field.
    Guise.   Come, follow me.
    Henry. Stay them! Stay, D'Ambois! Cousin Guise, I
      wonder
Your equal disposition brooks so ill
A man so good, that only would uphold   90
Man in his native noblesse, from whose fall

63 *headlong* rash   67 *charge* bout   69 (see p. 91)
74 *Hydra* the nine-headed monster slain by Hercules
76 (see p. 91)   77 *gradation* degree of rank
79 (see p. 91)   84 (see p. 91)
86 *duke* pun on dux, leader (see also p. 91)

All our dissensions rise; that in himself,
Without the outward patches of our frailty,
Riches and honour, knows he comprehends
95 Worth with the greatest: kings had never borne
Such boundless eminence over other men,
Had all maintained the spirit and state of D'Ambois;
Nor had the full impartial hand of Nature
That all things gave in her original,
100 Without these definite terms of Mine and Thine,
Been turned unjustly to the hand of Fortune,
Had all preserved her in her prime, like D'Ambois;
No envy, no disjunction had dissolved,
Or plucked out one stick of the golden faggot
105 In which the world of Saturn was comprised,
Had all been held together with the nerves,
The genius, and th' ingenuous soul of D'Ambois.
Let my hand therefore be the Hermean rod
To part and reconcile, and so conserve you,
110 As my combined embracers and supporters.
  Bussy. 'Tis our King's motion, and we shall not seem
To worst eyes womanish, though we change thus soon
Never so great grudge for his greater pleasure.
  Guise. I seal to that, and so the manly freedom
115 That you so much profess, hereafter prove not
A bold and glorious licence to deprave,
To me his hand shall prove the Hermean rod
His grace affects, in which submissive sign
On this his sacred right hand, I lay mine.
120 *Bussy*. 'Tis well, my lord, and so your worthy greatness
Engender not the greater insolence,
Nor make you think it a prerogative
To rack men's freedoms with the ruder wrongs,
My hand, stuck full of laurel, in true sign
125 'Tis wholly dedicate to righteous peace,
In all submission kisseth th' other side.
  Henry. Thanks to ye both; and kindly I invite ye
Both to a banquet, where we'll sacrifice
Full cups to confirmation of your loves;
130 At which, fair ladies, I entreat your presence.

94 *comprehends* comprises, contains
101 *turned to* i.e. turned into
105 *the world of Saturn* i.e. the Golden Age   108 (see p. 91)
110 (see p. 91)   123 *rack* torture

Exeunt HENRY, D'AMBOIS, [*and*] LADIES.

Monsieur. What had my bounty drunk when it raised
    him?
Guise. Y'ave stuck us up a very proper flag,
That takes more wind than we with all our sails.
    Monsieur. Oh, so he spreads and flourishes.
    Guise.   He must down,
Upstarts should never perch too near a crown.   135
    Monsieur. 'Tis true, my lord; and as this doting hand,
Even out of earth, like Juno, struck this giant,
So Jove's great ordnance shall be here implied
To strike him under th' Etna of his pride:
To which work lend your hands, and let us cast   140
Where we may set snares for his gadding greatness:
I think it best, amongst our greatest women;
For there is no such trap to catch an upstart
As a loose downfall; and indeed their falls
Are th' ends of all men's rising: if great men   145
And wise make scapes to please advantage
'Tis with a woman: women, that worst may,
Still hold men's candles: they direct and know
All things amiss in all men, and their women
All things amiss in them; through whose charmed mouths 150
We may see all the close scapes of the Court.
When the most royal beast of chase, being old
And cunning in his choice of lairs and haunts,
Can never be discovered to the bow,
The piece or hound, yet where his custom is   155
To beat his vault, and he ruts with his hind,
The place is marked, and by his venery
He still is taken. Shall we then attempt
The chiefest mean to that discovery here,
And court our greatest ladies' greatest women   160
With shows of love and liberal promises?
'Tis but our breath. If something given in hand
Sharpen their hopes of more, 'twill be well ventured.

---

131 (see p. 91)   136–9 (see p. 91)   138 *implied* employed
140 *cast* deliberate 141 *gadding* ranging 146 (see p. 91)
147–8 (see p. 91)   150 *charmed mouths* i.e. won over with gold
152 *the most royal beast of chase* i.e. the hart 152–6 (see p. 92)
155 *The piece* the fire-arm   156 (see p. 92)
157 *venery* the pursuit of sexual pleasure and also the sport of
    hunting

Guise. No doubt of that; and 'tis an excellent point
165 Of our devised investigation.
Monsieur. I have already broke the ice, my lord,
With the most trusted woman of your Countess,
And hope I shall wade through to our discovery.
Montsurry. Take say of her, my lord, she comes most fitly,
And we will to the other.

Enter CHARLOTTE, ANNABLE, PERO.

170 *Guise.*   Y'are engaged.
Annable. Nay, pray, my lord, forbear.
Montsurry. What, skittish, servant?
Annable. No, my lord, I am not so fit for your service.
Charlotte. Pray pardon me now, my lord; my lady
expects me.
175 *Guise.* I'll satisfy her expectation, as far as an uncle may.
Monsieur. Well said, a spirit of courtship of all hands!
Now, mine own Pero, hast thou remembered me for the
discovery I entreated thee to make concerning thy mistress?
Speak boldly, and be sure of all things I have promised.
180 *Pero.* Building on that you have sworn, my lord, I may
speak; and much the rather, because my lady hath not
trusted me with that I can tell you; for now I cannot be said
to betray her.
Monsieur. That's all one, so it be not to one that will
185 betray thee; forth, I beseech thee.
Pero. To tell you truth, my lord, I have made a strange
discovery.
Monsieur. Excellent Pero, thou revivest me; may I sink
quick into earth here if my tongue discover it.
190 *Pero.* 'Tis thus, then: this last night, my lord lay forth,
and I, wondering my lady's sitting up, stole at midnight
from my pallet, and, having before made a hole both through
the wall and arras to her inmost chamber, I saw D'Ambois
and she set close at a banquet.
195 *Monsieur.* D'Ambois?
Pero. Even he, my lord.
Monsieur. Dost thou not dream, wench?
Pero. No, my lord, he is the man.
Monsieur. The devil he is, and thy lady his dam! [Why,

169 *Take say* i.e. assay: make trial   170 (see p. 92)
175 *uncle.* Guise was uncle to Beaupré   189 *quick* alive
194 (see p. 92)   199–201 (see p. 92)

ammunition

this was the happiest shot that ever flew; the just plague of   200
hypocrisy levelled it. Oh, the] infinite regions betwixt a
woman's tongue and her heart! Is this our Goddess of
chastity? I thought I could not be so slighted, if she had not
her freight besides, and therefore plotted this with her
woman. Dear Pero, I will advance thee for ever; but tell   205
me now—God's precious, it transforms me with admiration
—sweet Pero, whom should she trust with his conveyance?
Or, all the doors being made sure, how could his conveyance be performed?

Pero. Nay, my lord, that amazes me; I cannot by any   210
study so much as guess at it.

Monsieur. Well, let's favour our apprehensions with for-
bearing that a little; for, if my heart were not hooped with
adamant, the conceit of this would have burst it. But hark
thee.   215

Whispers [to PERO].

Charlotte. I swear to your grace, all that I can conjecture
touching my lady your niece is a strong affection she bears
to the English Milor.

Guise. All, quod you? 'Tis enough, I assure you, but tell
me.

[whispers.]

Montsurry. I pray thee, resolve me: the Duke will never   220
imagine that I am busy about's wife: hath D'Ambois any
privy access to her?

Annable. No, my lord; D'Ambois neglects her, as she
takes it, and is therefore suspicious that either your Countess,
or the Lady Beaupré, hath closely entertained him.   225

Montsurry. By'r lady, a likely suspicion, and very near the
life, if she marks it—especially of my wife.

Monsieur [aside to PERO]. Come, we'll put off all with
seeming only to have courted.—Away, dry palm! Sh'as a
liver as hard as a biscuit; a man may go a whole voyage with   230
her, and get nothing but tempests at her wind-pipe.

Guise. Here's one, I think, has swallowed a porcupine,
she casts pricks from her tongue so.

Montsurry. And here's a peacock seems to have devoured

---

204 *freight* cargo   206 *admiration* wonder
213 (see p. 92)   214 *conceit* notion
218 *Milor* Milord. The French designation for an English gentleman
219 *quod you?* do you say?   224–5 (see p. 92)
228 *put off all* disguise all   229 (see p. 92)   230 (see p. 92)

235   one of the Alps, she has so swelling a spirit, and is so cold
of her kindness.

      Charlotte. We be no windfalls, my lord; ye must gather
us with the ladder of matrimony, or we'll hang till we be
rotten.

240   *Monsieur.* Indeed, that's the way to make ye right open-
arses. But, alas, ye have no portions fit for such husbands
as we wish you.

      Pero. Portions, my lord? yes, and such portions as your
principality cannot purchase.

245   *Monsieur.* What, woman, what are those portions?

      Pero. Riddle my riddle, my lord.

      Monsieur. Ay, marry wench, I think thy portion is a right
riddle; a man shall never find it out. But let's hear it.

      Pero. You shall, my lord.

250   *What's that, that being most rare's most cheap?*
         That if you sow, you never reap?
         That when it grows most, most you in it;
         And still you lose it when you win it?
         That when 'tis commonest, 'tis dearest,
255   *And when 'tis farthest off, 'tis nearest?*

      Monsieur. Is this your portion?

      Pero. Even this, my lord.

      Monsieur. Believe me, I cannot riddle it.

      Pero. No, my lord: 'tis my chastity, which you shall
260   neither riddle nor fiddle.

      Monsieur. Your chastity? Let me begin with the end of
you; how is a woman's chastity nearest a man when 'tis
farthest off?

      Pero. Why, my lord, when you cannot get it, it goes to th'
265   heart on you; and that, I think, comes most near you: and
I am sure it shall be far enough off; and so I leave you to
my mercy.   *Exeunt* WOMEN

      Monsieur. Farewell, riddle!

      Guise. Farewell, medlar!

270   *Montsurry.* Farewell, winter plum!

237 *windfalls* fruit which falls too easily
250–5 (see p. 92)
258 *riddle* pierce with holes like a riddle
265 *comes most near* bothers you, affects you most
270 (see pp. 92–3)

Monsieur. Now, my lords, what fruit of our inquisition?
Feel you nothing budding yet? Speak, good my lord
Montsurry.

Montsurry. Nothing but this: D'Ambois is negligent in
observing the Duchess, and therefore she is suspicious that   275
your niece or my wife closely entertains him.

Monsieur. Your wife, my lord? Think you that possible?

Montsurry. Alas, I know she flies him like her last hour.

Monsieur. Her last hour? Why, that comes upon her the
more she flies it. Does D'Ambois so, think you?   280

Montsurry. That's not worth the answering. 'Tis horrible
to think with what monsters women's imaginations engross
them when they are once enamoured, and what wonders
they will work for their satisfaction. They will make a sheep
valiant, a lion fearful.   285

Monsieur. And an ass confident, my lord, 'tis true, and
more will come forth shortly; get you to the banquet.

                              Exit GUISE *and* MONTSURRY
Oh, the unsounded sea of women's bloods,
That when 'tis calmest, is most dangerous!
Not any wrinkle creaming in their faces,   290
When in their hearts are Scylla and Charybdis,
Which still are hid in monster-formed clouds,
Where never day shines, nothing ever grows,
But weeds and poisons that no statesman knows:
Not Cerberus ever saw the damned nooks   295
Hid with the veil of women's virtuous looks.
I will conceal all yet, and give more time
To D'Ambois' trial, now upon my hook;
He awes my throat, else like Sybilla's cave
It should breathe oracles; I fear him strangely,   300
And may resemble his advanced valour
Unto a spirit raised without a circle,
Endangering him that ignorantly raised him,
And for whose fury he hath learned no limit.

276 *closely entertains* is intimate with him
282 *engross* occupy wholly; also, make gross
288 *unsounded* unfathomed
291 (see p. 93)   292 (see p. 93)
294 *statesman* such as even a politician does not know
295 *Cerberus* The three-headed watch-dog of Hades
296 (see p. 93)   299 (see p. 93)   301 (see p. 93)
302 (see p. 93)

Enter D'AMBOIS

How now, what leapest thou at?
305   *Bussy.*   O royal object!
    Monsieur. Thou dreamest awake; object in th'empty air?
    Bussy. Worthy the head of Titan, worth his chair.
    Monsieur. Pray thee, what meanest thou?
    Bussy.   See you not a crown
Impale the forehead of the great King Monsieur?
    Monsieur. O, fie upon thee!
310   *Bussy.*   Sir, that is the subject
Of all these your retired and sole discourses.
    Monsieur. Wilt thou not leave that wrongful supposition?
This still hath made me doubt thou dost not love me.
Wilt thou do one thing for me then sincerely?
315   *Bussy.* Ay, anything, but killing of the King.
    Monsieur. Still in that discord, and ill-taken note?
    Bussy. Come, do not doubt me, and command me all
        things.
    Monsieur. I will not, then; and now by all my love
Shown to thy virtues, and by all fruits else
320 Already sprung from that affection,
I charge thee utter, even with all the freedom
Both of thy noble nature and thy friendship,
The full and plain state of me in thy thoughts.
    Bussy. What, utter plainly what I think of you?
325 Why, this swims quite against the stream of greatness;
Great men would rather hear their flatteries,
And if they be not made fools, are not wise.
    Monsieur. I am no such great fool, and therefore charge
        thee
Even from the root of thy free heart, display me.
330   *Bussy.* Since you affect it in such serious terms,
If yourself first will tell me what you think
As freely and as heartily of me,
I'll be as open in my thoughts of you.
    Monsieur. A bargain, of mine honour! And make this,
335 That prove we in our full dissection
Never so foul, live still the sounder friends.

305 (see p. 93)
307 *chair* his seat in the chariot of the sun (see also p. 93)
309 *impale* encircle
311 *sole discourses* solitary communings (Parrott)
327 (see p. 93)   334 *make this* i.e. this bargain also
336 *live still* let us live still

Bussy. What else, sir? Come, begin, and speak me simply.
Monsieur. I will, I swear. I think thee then a man
That dares as much as a wild horse or tiger,
As headstrong and as bloody; and to feed   340
The ravenous wolf of thy most cannibal valour,
Rather than not employ it, thou wouldst turn
Hackster to any whore, slave to a Jew,
Or English usurer, to force possessions,
And cut men's throats of mortgaged estates;   345
Or thou wouldst tire thee like a tinker's wife
And murther market-folks; quarrel with sheep,
And run as mad as Ajax; serve a butcher;
Do anything but killing of the King:
That in thy valour th'art like other naturals   350
That have strange gifts in nature, but no soul
Diffused quite through, to make them of a piece,
But stop at humours, that are more absurd,
Childish, and villainous than that hackster, whore,
Slave, cut-throat, tinker's bitch, compared before;   355
And in those humours wouldst envy, betray,
Slander, blaspheme, change each hour a religion,
Do anything, but killing of the King:
That in thy valour—which is still the dunghill,
To which I carry all filth in thy house—   360
Th'art more ridiculous and vain-glorious
Than any mountebank, and impudent
Than any painted bawd; which not to soothe,
And glorify thee like a Jupiter Hammon,
Thou eat'st thy heart in vinegar, and thy gall   365
Turns all thy blood to poison, which is cause
Of that toad-pool that stands in thy complexion,
And makes thee, with a cold and earthy moisture,
Which is the dam of putrefaction,
As plague to thy damn'd pride, rot as thou liv'st,   370
To study calumnies and treacheries,
To thy friends' slaughters like a screech-owl sing,
And to all mischiefs, but to kill the King.

337 *simply* honestly, sincerely
343 *Hackster* cut-throat, swashbuckler   346 *tire* attire
348 (see pp. 93–4)
350 *natural* half-wits possessing strange and supernatural gifts
353 (see p. 94)   360 (see p. 94)   364 (see p. 94)
365 (see p. 94)   367 (see p. 94)
372 *screech-owl* bird of ill-omen, portending death

Bussy. So! Have you said?

Monsieur.   How think'st thou? Do I flatter?
375   Speak I not like a trusty friend to thee?

Bussy. That ever any man was blest withal;
So here's for me! I think you are at worst
No devil, since y'are like to be no king;
Of which, with any friend of yours I'll lay
380   This poor stillado here, gainst all the stars,
Ay, and gainst all your treacheries, which are more,
That you did never good, but to do ill;
But ill of all sorts, free and for itself:
That—like a murthering piece, making lanes in armies,
385 —The first man of a rank, the whole rank failing—
If you have wronged one man, y'are so far
From making him amends, that all his race,
Friends, and associates fall into your chase:
That y'are for perjuries the very prince
390   Of all intelligencers; and your voice
Is like an eastern wind, that, where it flies,
Knits nets of caterpillars, with which you catch
The prime of all the fruits the kingdom yields:
That your political head is the cursed fount
395   Of all the violence, rapine, cruelty,
Tyranny, and atheism flowing through the realm:
That y'ave a tongue so scandalous, 'twill cut
A perfect crystal; and a breath that will
Kill to that wall a spider; you will jest
400   With God, and your soul to the devil tender
For lust; kiss horror, and with death engender:
That your foul body is a Lernean fen
Of all the maladies breeding in all men;
That you are utterly without a soul;
405   And, for your life, the thread of that was spun
When Clotho slept, and let her breathing rock
Fall in the dirt; and Lachesis still draws it,
Dipping her twisting fingers in a bowl
Defiled, and crowned with virtue's forced soul:
410   And lastly, which I must for gratitude
Ever remember, that of all my height

---

380 *stillado* perhaps 'stiletto'   384 *murthering piece* a cannon
390 *intelligencers* informers, spies
394 *political* concerned with policy   401 (see p. 94)
402 *Lernean fen* home of the Hydra killed by Hercules
406–7 (see p. 94)   411 *height* high advancement

And dearest life you are the only spring,
Only in royal hope to kill the King.
    Monsieur. Why, now I see thou lovest me; come to the
      banquet.   *Exeunt*

Act IV, Scene i

HENRY, MONSIEUR *with a letter*, GUISE, MONTSURRY,
    BUSSY, ELENOR, TAMYRA, BEAUPRÉ, PERO, CHARLOTTE,
    ANNABLE, PYRHA, *with four* PAGES.

    Henry. Ladies, ye have not done our banquet right,
Nor looked upon it with those cheerful rays
That lately turned your breaths to floods of gold;
Your looks, methinks, are not drawn out with thoughts
So clear and free as heretofore, but fare   5
As if the thick complexions of men
Governed within them.
    Bussy.   'Tis not like, my lord,
That men in women rule, but contrary;
For as the moon of all things God created
Not only is the most appropriate image   10
Or glass to show them how they wax and wane,
But in her light and motion likewise bears
Imperial influences that command
In all their powers, and make them wax and wane;
So women, that of all things made of nothing   15
Are the most perfect images of the moon,
Or still-unweaned sweet moon-calves with white faces,
Not only are patterns of change to men,
But, as the tender moonshine of their beauties
Clears or is cloudy, make men glad or sad.   20
    Monsieur. But here the moons are changed, as the King
      notes,
And either men rule in them, or some power
Beyond their voluntary motions,
For nothing can recover their lost faces.
    Bussy. None can be always one: our griefs and joys   25
Hold several sceptres in us, and have times
For their predominance: which grief now in them
Doth claim as proper to his diadem.

6 *thick complexions* clouded; refers to the mixture of humours
9–20 (see pp. 94–5)   17 (see p. 95)

And grief's a natural sickness of the blood,
30   That time to part asks, as his coming had;
Only slight fools, grieved, suddenly are glad;
A man may say t' a dead man, 'Be revived,'
As well as to one sorrowful, 'Be not grieved.'
And therefore, princely mistress, in all wars   *clear*
                                   [*To the* DUCHESS]
35 ⸱ Against these base foes that insult on weakness,
And still fight housed behind the shield of Nature,
Of tyrannous law, treachery, or beastly need,
Your servant cannot help; authority here
Goes with corruption, something like some States
40   That back worst men: valour to them must creep
That, to themselves left, would fear him asleep.
      Duchess. Ye all take that for granted that doth rest
Yet to be proved; we all are as we were,
As merry and as free in thought as ever.
45   *Guise*. And why then can ye not disclose your thoughts?
      Tamyra. Methinks the man hath answered for us well.
      Monsieur. The man? Why, madam, d'ye not know his
            name?
      Tamyra. Man is a name of honour for a king:
Additions take away from each chief thing.
50   The school of modesty not to learn learns dames:
They sit in high forms there, that know men's names.
      Monsieur.—Hark, sweetheart, here's a bound set to your
            valour!
It cannot enter here, no, not to notice
Of what your name is; your great eagle's beak,
55   Should you fly at her, had as good encounter
An Albion cliff, as her more craggy liver.
      Bussy. I'll not attempt her, sir; her sight and name,
By which I only know her, doth deter me.
      Henry. So they do all men else.
      Monsieur.   You would say so
If you knew all.
60   *Tamyra*.   Knew all, my lord? What mean you?
      Monsieur. All that I know, madam.
      Tamyra.   That you know? Speak it.
      Monsieur. No, 'tis enough I feel it.

35 (see p. 95)   37 (see p. 95)   48–51 (see p. 95)
49 *Additions* further titles
51 *in high forms* i.e. on dunces' stools for their immodesty
52–6 (see pp. 95–6)   59 (see p. 96)

Henry.   But, methinks
Her courtship is more pure than heretofore;
True courtiers should be modest, but not nice,
Bold, but not impudent, pleasure love, not vice.   65
    Monsieur.—Sweetheart, come hither! What if one should
        make
Horns at Montsurry? Would it strike him jealous
Through all the proofs of his chaste lady's virtues?
    Bussy. No, I think not.
    Monsieur. Not if I named the man
With whom I would make him suspicious   70
His wife hath armed his forehead?
    Bussy.   So you might
Have your great nose made less indeed, and slit,
Your eyes thrust out.
    Monsieur.   Peace, peace, I pray thee peace.
Who dares do that? The brother of his King?
    Bussy. Were your King brother in you; all your powers,   75
Stretched in the arms of great men and their bawds,
Set close down by you; all your stormy laws
Spouted with lawyers' mouths, and gushing blood,
Like to so many torrents; all your glories,
Making you terrible, like enchanted flames   80
Fed with bare cockscombs and with crooked hams;
All your prerogatives, your shames and tortures;
All daring heaven, and opening hell about you—
Were I the man ye wronged so and provoked,
Though ne'er so much beneath you, like a box-tree   85
I would, out of the toughness of my root,
Ram hardness in my lowness and, like Death
Mounted on earthquakes, I would trot through all
Honours and horrors; through foul and fair,
And from your whole strength toss you into air.   90
    Monsieur. Go, th'art a devil! Such another spirit
Could not be stilled from all th' Armenian dragons.
O my love's glory, heir to all I have,
—That's all I can say, and that all I swear—
If thou outlive me, as I know thou must,   95
Or else hath Nature no proportioned end
To her great labours; she hath breathed a spirit
Into thy entrails, of effect to swell

---

64 *nice* over-fastidious   71 (see p. 96)   76 (see p. 96)
81 (see p. 96)   85 (see p. 96)   87 *Ram* stuff into
92 *stilled* distilled (see also p. 96)   96 (see p. 96)

Into another great Augustus Cæsar,
100   Organs and faculties fitted to her greatness;
And should that perish like a common spirit,
Nature's a courtier and regards no merit.

    Henry. Here's nought but whispering with us; like a calm
Before a tempest, when the silent air
105   Lays her soft ear close to the earth to hearken
For that she fears is coming to afflict her;
Some fate doth join our ears to hear it coming.
Come, my brave eagle, let's to covert fly;
I see Almighty Æther in the smoke
110   Of all his clouds descending, and the sky
Hid in the dim ostents of tragedy.

Exit HENRY *with* D'AMBOIS *and* LADIES.

    Guise [*aside to* MONSIEUR]. Now stir the humour, and
begin the brawl.
    Montsurry. The King and D'Ambois now are grown all
      one.
    Monsieur [*making horns at* MONTSURRY]. Nay, they are two,
      my lord.
    Montsurry. How's that?
    Monsieur.   No more.
    Montsurry. I must have more, my lord.
115   *Monsieur.*   What, more than two?
    Montsurry. How monstrous is this!
    Monsieur.   Why?
    Montsurry.   You make me horns!
    Monsieur. Not I, it is a work without my power;
Married men's ensigns are not made with fingers;
Of divine fabric they are, not men's hands;
120   Your wife, you know, is a mere Cynthia,
And she must fashion horns out of her nature.
    Montsurry. But doth she? Dare you charge her? Speak,
      false prince.
    Monsieur. I must not speak, my lord; but if you'll use
The learning of a nobleman, and read,
125   Here's something to those points; soft, you must pawn
Your honour having read it to return it.

Enter TAMYRA, PERO.

---

109 *Almighty Æther* Jove   112 *brawl*, a dance, as well as a row
117 *without* outside, beyond   118 *ensign* heraldic emblem
120 (see p. 96)   125-7 (see p. 96)

Montsurry. Not I! I pawn mine honour for a paper?
Monsieur. You must not buy it under.

                      Exeunt GUISE *and* MONSIEUR.

Montsurry.   Keep it then,
And keep fire in your bosom.
    Tamyra.   What says he?
    Montsurry. You must make good the rest.
    Tamyra.   How fares my lord?   130
Takes my love anything to heart he says?
    Montsurry. Come y'are a—
    Tamyra.   What, my lord?
    Montsurry.   The plague of Herod
Feast in his rotten entrails.
    Tamyra.   Will you wreak
Your anger's just cause given by him, on me?
    Montsurry. By him?
    Tamyra.   By him, my lord; I have admired   135
You could all this time be at concord with him,
That still hath played such discords on your honour.
    Montsurry. Perhaps 'tis with some proud string of my
      wife's.
    Tamyra. How's that, my lord?
    Montsurry.   Your tongue will still admire,
Till my head be the miracle of the world.   140
    Tamyra. Oh, woe is me!

                      She seems to swound.
    Pero.   What does your lordship mean?
Madam, be comforted; my lord but tries you.
Madam! Help, good my lord, are you not moved?
Do your set looks print in your words your thoughts?
Sweet lord, clear up those eyes, for shame of noblesse;   145
Merciless creature! But it is enough,
You have shot home, your words are in her heart;
She has not lived to bear a trial now.
    Montsurry. Look up, my love, and by this kiss receive
My soul amongst thy spirits, for supply   150
To thine chased with my fury.
    Tamyra.   Oh, my lord,
I have too long lived to hear this from you.
    Montsurry. 'Twas from my troubled blood, and not from
      me.

132 *The Plague of Herod* Acts, XII, 23. The plague of worms
135 *admired* wondered   138 proud: wanton, on heat
144 (see p. 96)   149–58 (see pp. 96–7)

—I know not how I fare; a sudden night
155 Flows through my entrails, and a headlong chaos
Murmurs within me, which I must digest,
And not drown her in my confusions,
That was my life's joy, being best informed.—
Sweet, you must needs forgive me, that my love,
160 Like to a fire disdaining his suppression,
Raged being discouraged; my whole heart is wounded
When any least thought in you is but touched,
And shall be till I know your former merits,
Your name and memory, altogether crave
165 In loathed oblivion their eternal grave;
And then, you must hear from me, there's no mean
In any passion I shall feel for you;
Love is a razor cleansing, being well used,
But fetcheth blood still, being the least abused;
170 To tell you briefly all—the man that left me
When you appeared, did turn me worse than woman,
And stabbed me to the heart thus [*making horns*], with his
            hand.
      Tamyra. Oh, happy woman! Comes my stain from him?
It is my beauty, and that innocence proves
175 That slew Chimæra, rescued Peleus
From all the savage beasts in Pelion,
And raised the chaste Athenian prince from hell:
All suffering with me, they for women's lusts,
I for a man's, that the Augean stable
180 Of his foul sin would empty in my lap.
How his guilt shunned me! Sacred Innocence,
That where thou fear'st art dreadful, and his face
Turned in flight from thee, that had thee in chase;
Come, bring me to him; I will tell the serpent
185 Even to his teeth whence, in mine honour's soil,
A pitched field starts up 'twixt my lord and me,
That his throat lies, and he shall curse his fingers,
For being so governed by his filthy soul.
      Montsurry. I know not if himself will vaunt t'have been
190 The princely author of the slavish sin,

---

166 *mean* moderation   174 (see p. 97)
175 (see p. 97)   177 (see p. 97)
179 *the Augean stables* the cleaning of which was Hercules' sixth
      labour
181–3 (see p. 97)   184–6 (see p. 97)
187 *fingers* the horns referred to in line 172

Or any other; he would have resolved me,
Had you not come, not by his word, but writing,
Would I have sworn to give it him again,
And pawned mine honour to him for a paper.
    Tamyra. See how he flies me still! 'Tis a foul heart   195
That fears his own hand. Good, my lord, make haste
To see the dangerous paper; be not nice
For any trifle, jewelled with your honour,
To pawn your honour; and with it confer
My nearest woman here in all she knows,   200
Who, if the sun or Cerberus could have seen
Any stain in me, might as much as they;
And, Pero, here I charge thee by my love,
And all proofs of it, which I might call bounties,
By all that thou hast seen seem good in me,   205
And all the ill which thou shouldst spit from thee,
By pity of the wound my Lord hath given me,
Not as thy mistress now, but a poor woman,
To death given over, rid me of my pains;
Pour on thy powder; clear thy breast of me: 210
My lord is only here; here speak thy worst,
Thy best will do me mischief; if thou spar'st me,
Never shine good thought on thy memory!
Resolve my lord, and leave me desperate.
    Pero. My lord!—My lord hath played a prodigal's part,   215
To break his stock for nothing; and an insolent,
To cut a Gordian when he could not loose it:
What violence is this, to put true fire
To a false train, to blow up long-crowned peace
With sudden outrage, and believe a man   220
Sworn to the shame of women, gainst a woman
Born to their honours! I'll attend your lordship.
    Tamyra. No, I will write—for I shall never more
Speak with the fugitive—where I will defy him,
Were he ten times the brother of my king.   225
                        Exeunt.

197 (see p. 98)
199 *confer* a combination of 'compare' and 'consult' (Brooke)
201 (see p. 98)   210 (see p. 98)   216 (see p. 98)
217 (see p. 98)   218–19 (see p. 98)   222 (see p. 98)

Act IV, Scene ii

Music. TAMYRA *enters with* PERO, *her maid, bearing a letter.*

Tamyra. Away, deliver it.   *Exit* PERO.
                   Oh, may my lines,
Filled with the poison of a woman's hate,
When he shall open them, shrink up his eyes
With torturous darkness, such as stands in hell,
5   Stuck full of inward horrors, never lighted,
With which are all things to be feared, affrighted—
              Bussy ascends with the Friar.
Father!
    Bussy. How is it with my honoured mistress?
    Tamyra. O servant, help, and save me from the gripes
Of shame and infamy.
    Bussy.   What insensate stock
10   Or rude inanimate vapour without fashion,
Durst take into his Epimethean breast
A box of such plagues as the danger yields
Incurred in this discovery? He had better
Ventured his breast in the consuming reach
15   Of the hot surfeits cast out of the clouds,
Or stood the bullets that, to wreak the sky,
The Cyclops ram in Jove's artillery.
    Friar. We soon will take the darkness from his face
That did that deed of darkness; we will know
20   What now the Monsieur and your husband do,
What is contained within the secret paper
Offered by Monsieur, and your love's events:
To which ends, honoured daughter, at your motion,
I have put on these exorcising rites,
25   And, by my power of learned holiness
Vouchsafed me from above, I will command
Our resolution of a raised spirit.
    Tamyra. Good father, raise him in some beauteous form,
That with least terror I may brook his sight.

s.d. (see p. 98)   6 (see p. 98)
  9 *insensate stock* unfeeling senseless block of wood
  10 *rude* unformed, unfinished; *fashion* form
  11 (see p. 98)   15 *hot surfeits* lightning
  16 (see p. 98)   22 *events* outcome
  27 *our resolution* the resolution of our doubts (see also pp. 98–9)

Friar. Stand sure together, then, whate'er ye see,   30
And stir not, as ye tender all our lives.

He puts on his robes.

*Occidentalium legionum spiritualium imperator (magnus
ille Behemoth) veni, veni, comitatus cum Astaroth locotenente
invicto. Adjuro te per Stygis inscrutabilia arcana, per ipsos
irremeabiles anfractus Averni: adesto ô Behemoth, tu cui*   35
*pervia sunt Magnatum scrinia; veni, per Noctis & tenebrarum
abdita profundissima; per labentia sidera; per ipsos motus
horarum furtivos, Hecatesque altum silentium! Appare in
forma spiritali, lucente, splendida & amabili.*

Thunder. [BEHEMOTH *rises. Enter* CARTOPHYLAX, *etc.*]

Behemoth. What would the holy Friar?
Friar.   .   I would see   40
What now the Monsieur and Montsurry do,
And see the secret paper that the Monsieur
Offered to Count Montsurry, longing much
To know on what events the secret loves
Of these two honoured persons shall arrive.   45
Behemoth. Why call'dst thou me to this accursed light,
To these light purposes? I am Emperor
Of that inscrutable darkness where are hid
All deepest truths, and secrets never seen,
All which I know, and command legions   50
Of knowing spirits that can do more than these.
Any of this my guard that circle me
In these blue fires, and out of whose dim fumes
Vast murmurs use to break, and from their sounds
Articulate voices, can do ten parts more   55
Than open such slight truths as you require.
Friar. From the last night's black depth I called up one
Of the inferior ablest ministers,
And he could not resolve me; send one then
Out of thine own command, to fetch the paper   60
That Monsieur hath to show to Count Montsurry.
Behemoth. I will. Cartophylax, thou that properly
Hast in thy power all papers so inscribed,
Glide through all bars to it and fetch that paper.
Cartophylax. I will.   *A torch removes.*

31 *tender* value   32–9 (see p. 99)
39 s.d. *Cartophylax* 'Guardian of papers'
54 *use to* are used to, i.e. continually break   64 s.d. (see p. 99)

65   *Friar.*   Till he returns, great Prince of Darkness,
Tell me if Monsieur and the Count Montsurry
Are yet encountered.
        Behemoth.   Both them and the Guise
Are now together.
        Friar.   Show us all their persons,
And represent the place, with all their actions.
70   *Behemoth.* The spirit will straight return, and then I'll
        show thee.
                            [*The torch returns.*]
See, he is come. Why brought'st thou not the paper?
        Cartophylax. He hath prevented me, and got a spirit
Raised by another great in our command,
To take the guard of it before I came.
75;   *Behemoth.* This is your slackness, not t' invoke our powers
When first your acts set forth to their effects;
Yet shall you see it and themselves: behold
They come here, and the Earl now holds the paper.

        Enter MONSIEUR, GUISE, MONTSURRY, *with a paper.*

        Bussy. May we not hear them?
        [*Friar.*]   No, be still and see.
        Bussy. I will go fetch the paper.
80   *Friar.*   Do not stir;
There's too much distance and too many locks
'Twixt you and them, how near soe'er they seem,
For any man to interrupt their secrets.
        Tamyra. O honoured spirit, fly into the fancy
85 Of my offended lord, and do not let him
Believe what there the wicked man hath written.
        Behemoth. Persuasion hath already entered him
Beyond reflection; peace till their departure.
        Monsieur. There is a glass of ink wherein you see
90 How to make ready black-faced tragedy:
You now discern, I hope, through all her paintings,
Her gasping wrinkles and fame's sepulchres.
        Guise. Think you he feigns, my lord? What hold you now?
Do we malign your wife, or honour you?
        Monsieur. What, stricken dumb! Nay fie, lord, be not
95   daunted;
Your case is common; were it ne'er so rare,

72 *prevented* come before   73 (see p. 99)   79 (see p. 99)
84 (see p. 99)   88 *reflection* turning back
89 (see p. 99)   91 (see p. 99)   92 (see p. 99)

Bear it as rarely! Now to laugh were manly;
A worthy man should imitate the weather
That sings in tempests, and, being clear, is silent.

   Guise. Go home, my lord, and force your wife to write   100
Such loving stuff to D'Ambois as she used
When she desired his presence.

   Monsieur.   Do, my lord,
And make her name her concealed messenger,
That close and most inenarrable pander,
That passeth all our studies to exquire;   105
By whom convey the letter to her love;
And so you shall be sure to have him come
Within the thirsty reach of your revenge;
Before which, lodge an ambush in her chamber
Behind the arras, of your stoutest men   110
All close and soundly armed; and let them share
A spirit amongst them that would serve a thousand.

Enter PERO *with a letter.*

   Guise. Yet stay a little; see, she sends for you.
   Monsieur. Poor, loving lady; she'll make all good yet,
Think you not so, my lord?

MONTSURRY *stabs* PERO *and exit.*

   Guise.   Alas, poor soul!   115
   Monsieur. This was ill done, i' faith.
   Pero.   'Twas nobly done,
And I forgive his lordship from my soul.
   Monsieur. Then much good do't thee, Pero! Hast a letter?
   Pero. I hope it be, at least, if not a volume
Of worthy curses for your perjury.   120
   Monsieur. Now, out upon her.
   Guise.   Let me see, my lord,
   Monsieur. You shall presently. How fares my Pero?
Who's there?

Enter SERVANT.

        Take in this maid, sh'as caught a clap,
And fetch my surgeon to her; come, my lord,
We'll now peruse our letter.

---

104 *inenarrable* indescribable
105 *passeth* surpasseth; *exquire* search out   112 s.d. (see p. 100)
123 *clap* a blow, but also a form of venereal disease

Exeunt MONSIEUR, GUISE.

125   *Pero.*   Furies rise
Out of the black lines, and torment his soul.
                                   Lead her out.

    Tamyra. Hath my lord slain my woman?
    Behemoth.   No, she lives.
    Friar. What shall become of us?
    Behemoth.   All I can say,
Being called thus late, is brief, and darkly this:
130   If D'Ambois' mistress stain not her white hand
With his forced blood, he shall remain untouched;
So, father, shall yourself, but by yourself:
To make this augury plainer, when the voice
Of D'Ambois shall invoke me, I will rise,
135   Shining in greater light, and show him all
That will betide ye all; meantime be wise,
And let him curb his rage with policy.
           [He descends with his spirits.]
    Bussy. Will he appear to me when I invoke him?
    Friar. He will, be sure.
    Bussy.   It must be shortly then;
140   For his dark words have tied my thoughts on knots
Till he dissolve, and free them.
    Tamyra.   In meantime,
Dear servant, till your powerful voice revoke him,
Be sure to use the policy he advised;
Lest fury in your too quick knowledge taken
145   Of our abuse, and your defence of me,
Accuse me more than any enemy;
And, father, you must on my lord impose
Your holiest charges, and the Church's power
To temper his hot spirit and disperse
150   The cruelty and the blood I know his hand
Will shower upon our heads, if you put not
Your finger to the storm, and hold it up,
As my dear servant here must do with Monsieur.
    Bussy. I'll soothe his plots, and strow my hate with smiles,
155   Till all at once the close mines of my heart
Rise at full date, and rush into his blood:

129 *darkly* obscurely   130 (see p. 100)
132 *but by yourself* except by yourself   142 *revoke* call back
144–6 (see p. 100)   154 (see p. 100)
156 *at full date* when their proper time has elapsed

I'll bind his arm in silk, and rub his flesh,
To make the vein swell, that his soul may gush
Into some kennel where it longs to lie,
And policy shall be flanked with policy.   160
Yet shall the feeling centre where we meet
Groan with the weight of my approaching feet;
I'll make th' inspired threshals of his court
Sweat with the weather of my horrid steps,
Before I enter; yet will I appear   165
Like calm security before a ruin;
A politician must like lightning melt
The very marrow, and not print the skin:
His ways must not be seen; the superficies
Of the green centre must not taste his feet,   170
When hell is ploughed up with his wounding tracts,
And all his harvest reaped from hellish facts.   *Exeunt.*

Act V, Scene i

MONTSURRY, *bare, unbraced, pulling* TAMYRA *in by the hair,*
FRIAR. *One bearing light, a standish and paper, which sets a
table.*

    Friar. My lord, remember that your soul must seek
Her peace, as well as your revengeful blood;
You ever to this hour have proved yourself
A noble, zealous, and obedient son
T'our holy mother; be not an apostate: 5
Your wife's offence serves not, were it the worst
You can imagine, without greater proofs
To sever your eternal bonds and hearts;
Much less to touch her with a bloody hand:
Nor is it manly, much less husbandly,   10
To expiate any frailty in your wife
With churlish strokes or beastly odds of strength:
The stony birth of clouds will touch no laurel,
Nor any sleeper; your wife is your laurel,

159 *kennel* gutter   160 (see p. 100)   161 (see p. 100)
163 (see p. 100)   169 (see p. 100)   V, i (see p. 100)
s.d. *bare* bare-headed; *unbraced*; not fully dressed;
    standish stand containing pens, ink, etc.
    13   (see p. 100)

15 And sweetest sleeper; do not touch her then;
    Be not more rude than the wild seed of vapour
    To her that is more gentle than it rude;
    In whom kind nature suffered one offence
    But to set off her other excellence.
20   *Montsurry.* Good father, leave us; interrupt no more
    The course I must run for mine honour sake.
    Rely on my love to her, which her fault
    Cannot extinguish; will she but disclose
    Who was the hateful minister of her love,
25 And through what maze he served it, we are friends.
        Friar. It is a damned work to pursue those secrets,
    That would ope more sin, and prove springs of slaughter;
    Nor is't a path for Christian feet to touch,
    But out of all way to the health of souls,
30 A sin impossible to be forgiven;
    Which he that dares commit—
        Montsurry.   Good father, cease;
    Tempt not a man distracted; I am apt
    To outrages that I shall ever rue!
    I will not pass the verge that bounds a Christian,
35 Nor break the limits of a man nor husband.
        Friar. Then God inspire ye both with thoughts and deeds
    Worthy his high respect, and your own souls.
                                    Exit Friar.
    Montsurry. Who shall remove the mountain from my
            heart,
    Ope the seven times-heat furnace of my thoughts,
40 And set fit outcries for a soul in hell?
                        MONTSURRY *turns a key.*
    O now it nothing fits my cares to speak
    But thunder, or to take into my throat
    The trump of Heaven, with whose determinate blasts
    The winds shall burst, and the enraged seas
45 Be drunk up in his sounds; that my hot woes,
    Vented enough, I might convert to vapour,
    Ascending from my infamy unseen,
    Shorten the world, preventing the last breath
    That kills the living, and regenerates death.
50   *Tamyra.* My lord, my fault, as you may censure it
    With too strong arguments, is past your pardon:
    But how the circumstances may excuse me

38–40 (see p. 100)   40 (see p. 101)   41 (see p. 101)
43 *determinate* bringing to an end   43–9 (see p. 101)

God knows, and your more temperate mind hereafter
May let my penitent miseries make you know.
    Montsurry. Hereafter? 'Tis a supposed infinite,   55
That from this point will rise eternally:
Fame grows in going; in the scapes of virtue
Excuses damn her: they be fires in cities
Enraged with those winds that less lights extinguish.
Come, Siren, sing, and dash against my rocks   60
Thy ruffian galley, [rigged with quench for lust!]
Sing, and put all the nets into thy voice
With which thou drewest into thy strumpet's lap
The spawn of Venus, and in which ye danced;
That, in thy lap's stead, I may dig his tomb,   65
And quit his manhood with a woman's sleight,
Who never is deceived in her deceit.
Sing (that is, write), and then take from mine eyes
The mists that hide the most inscrutable pander
That ever lapped up an adulterous vomit;   70
That I may see the devil, and survive
To be a devil, and then learn to wive:
That I may hang him, and then cut him down,
Then cut him up, and with my soul's beams search
The cranks and caverns of his brain, and study   75
The errant wilderness of a woman's face,
Where men cannot get out, for all the comets
That have been lighted at it: though they know
That adders lie a-sunning in their smiles,
That basilisks drink their poison from their eyes,   80
And no way there to coast out to their hearts;
Yet still they wander there, and are not stayed
Till they be fettered, nor secure before
All cares distract them, nor in human state
Till they embrace within their wife's two breasts   85
All Pelion and Cythaeron with their beasts.
Why write you not?
    Tamyra.   O, good my lord, forbear

55 (see p. 101)   57 (see p. 101)   57–9 (see p. 101)
60 (see p. 101)   61 (see p. 101)   62–5 (see p. 101)
66 (see pp. 101–2)   67 (see p. 102)   70 (see p. 102)
71–2 (see p. 102)   73–4 (see p. 102)
75 *cranks* winding paths   77 (see p. 102)
80 (see p. 102)   81 (see p. 102)
82 *stayed* halted, made still. Perhaps also, supported, comforted
    Cf. 'secure' (line 83).
84 (see p. 102)   86 (see p. 102)

In wreak of great sins to engender greater,
And make my love's corruption generate murther.

90   *Montsurry.* It follows needfully as child and parent;
The chain-shot of thy lust is yet aloft,
And it must murther; 'tis thine own dear twin:
No man can add height to a woman's sin.
Vice never doth her just hate so provoke,

95   As when she rageth under virtue's cloak.
Write! For it must be; by this ruthless steel,
By this impartial torture, and the death
Thy tyrannies have invented in my entrails,
To quicken life in dying, and hold up

100   The spirits in fainting, teaching to preserve
Torments in ashes, that will ever last.
Speak! Will you write?

        Tamyra.   Sweet lord, enjoin my sin
Some other penance than what makes it worse:
Hide in some gloomy dungeon my loathed face,

105   And let condemned murtherers let me down,
Stopping their noses, my abhorred food.
Hang me in chains, and let me eat these arms
That have offended: bind me face to face
To some dead woman, taken from the cart

110   Of execution, till death and time
In grains of dust dissolve me; I'll endure:
Or any torture that your wrath's invention
Can fright all pity from the world withal:
But to betray a friend with show of friendship,

115   That is too common for the rare revenge
Your rage affecteth; here then are my breasts,
Last night your pillows; here my wretched arms,
As late the wished confines of your life:
Now break them as you please, and all the bounds

120   Of manhood, noblesse, and religion.

        Montsurry. Where all these have been broken, they are
            kept
In doing their justice there; thine arms have lost
Their privilege in lust, and in their torture
Thus they must pay it.   *Stabs her.*

        Tamyra.   O Lord!

        Montsurry.   Till thou writ'st,

---

91 *chain-shot* cannon balls joined by chain   96–7 (see p. 102)
98 *tyrannies* lawless actions   99 (see p. 102)
113 *withal* with   121–2 (see p. 103)

I'll write in wounds, my wrong's fit characters,   125
Thy right of sufferance. Write!
    Tamyra.   Oh, kill me, kill me!
Dear husband, be not crueller than death;
You have beheld some Gorgon; feel, oh, feel
How you are turned to stone; with my heart-blood
Dissolve yourself again, or you will grow   130
Into the image of all tyranny.
    Montsurry. As thou art of adultery; I will still
Prove thee my like in ill, being most a monster;
Thus I express thee yet.   *Stabs her again.*
    Tamyra.   And yet I live.
    Montsurry. Ay, for thy monstrous idol is not done yet: 133
This tool hath wrought enough; now, Torture, use
This other engine on th' habituate powers
Of her thrice-damned and whorish fortitude.

    Enter SERVANTS [*and place* TAMYRA *on the rack*].

Use the most madding pains in her that ever
Thy venoms soaked through, making most of death,   140
That she may weigh her wrongs with them, and then
Stand, Vengeance, on thy steepest rock, a victor!
    Tamyra. Oh, who is turned into my lord and husband?
Husband! My lord! None but my lord and husband!
Heaven, I ask thee remission of my sins,   145
Not of my pains; husband, oh, help me, husband!

    The FRIAR *ascends with a sword drawn.*

    Friar. What rape of honour and religion!
Oh, wrack of nature!   *Falls and dies.*
    Tamyra.   Poor man! Oh, my father!
Father, look up! Oh, let me down, my lord,
And I will write.
    Montsurry.   Author of prodigies!   150
What new flame breaks out of the firmament,
That turns up counsels never known before?

---

125 *characters* letters   126 (see p. 103)
128 *Gorgon* Medusa whose head turned to stone any man who saw
    it
130 (see p. 103)   132–4 (see p. 103)   135 (see p. 103)
137 *habituate* having become habitual
140 (see p. 103)   146 (see p. 103)   148 (see pp. 103–4)
150 *prodigies* omens, portents such as comets: hence 'What new
    flame . . . ?'

Now is it true, earth moves, and heaven stands still;
Even heaven itself must see and suffer ill:
155 The too huge bias of the world hath swayed
Her back-part upwards, and with that she braves
This hemisphere, that long her mouth hath mocked!
The gravity of her religious face,
Now grown too weighty with her sacrilege
160 And here discerned sophisticate enough,
Turns to th' Antipodes; and all the forms
That her illusions have impressed in her,
Have eaten through her back; and now all see
How she is riveted with hypocrisy.
165 Was this the way? Was he the mean betwixt you?
    Tamyra. He was, he was, kind innocent man, he was.
    Montsurry. Write, write a word or two.
    Tamyra.   I will, I will.
I'll write, but in my blood, that he may see
These lines come from my wounds, and not from me.
                                        Writes.

    Montsurry. Well might he die for thought: methinks the
170   frame
And shaken joints of the whole world should crack
To see her parts so disproportionate;
And that his general beauty cannot stand
Without these stains in the particular man.
175 Why wander I so far? Here, here was she
That was a whole world without spot to me,
Though now a world of spots; oh, what a lightning
Is man's delight in women! What a bubble
He builds his state, fame, life on, when he marries!
180 Since all earth's pleasures are so short and small,
The way t'enjoy it, is t'abjure it all.
Enough! I must be messenger myself,
Disguised like this strange creature: in, I'll after,
To see what guilty light gives this cave eyes,
185 And to the world sing new impieties.

    Exeunt [SERVANTS]. *He puts the* FRIAR *in the vault and
    follows. She wraps herself in the arras.*

153 (see p. 104)
160 *sophisticate* adulterated, fallen from its original purity
162 *illusions* deceptions   165 *mean* go-between
173 (see p. 104)   184 *cave* i.e. the vault

Act V, Scene ii

[*Enter*] BUSSY D'AMBOIS *with two* PAGES.

Bussy. Sit up to-night, and watch; I'll speak with none
But the old friar, who bring to me.
Pages.   We will, sir.   *Exeunt.*
Bussy. What violent heat is this? Methinks the fire
Of twenty lives doth on a sudden flash
Through all my faculties: the air goes high   5
In this close chamber, and the frighted earth

                              Thunder.

Trembles, and shrinks beneath me; the whole house
Cracks with his shaken burthen.
                    Enter the FRIAR'S *ghost.*
                              Bless me, heaven!
Ghost. Note what I want, my son, and be forewarned:
Oh, there are bloody deeds past and to come.   10
I cannot stay; a fate doth ravish me;
I'll meet thee in the chamber of thy love.   *Exit.*
Bussy. What dismal change is here! The good old Friar
Is murthered, being made known to serve my love;
Note what he wants? He wants his utmost weed,   15
He wants his life and body: which of these
Should be the want he means, and may supply me
With any fit forewarning? This strange vision,
Together with the dark prediction
Used by the Prince of Darkness that was raised   20
By this embodied shadow, stir my thoughts
With reminiscion of the Spirit's promise,
Who told me that by any invocation
I should have power to raise him, though it wanted
The powerful words and decent rites of art.   25
Never had my set brain such need of spirit
T'instruct and cheer it; now then I will claim
Performance of his free and gentle vow
T'appear in greater light, and make more plain
His rugged oracle: I long to know   30

V, ii (see p. 104)   5–7 (see p. 104)   9 *want* lack
15 (see p. 104)
21 *this embodied shadow* this ghost when it was a living man
22 *reminiscion* recollection
26 *set* resolute (see also p. 104)   28 (see p. 104)

How my dear mistress fares, and be informed
What hand she now holds on the troubled blood
Of her incensed lord: methought the Spirit,
When he had uttered his perplexed presage,
35   Threw his changed countenance headlong into clouds;
His forehead bent, as it would hide his face,
He knocked his chin against his darkened breast,
And struck a churlish silence through his powers.
Terror of darkness! O thou King of flames!
40   That with thy music-footed horse dost strike
The clear light out of crystal on dark earth,
And hurlest instructive fire about the world,
Wake, wake the drowsy and enchanted night,
That sleeps with dead eyes in this heavy riddle!
45   Or thou great Prince of shades where never sun
Sticks his far-darted beams, whose eyes are made
To see in darkness, and see ever best
Where sense is blindest, open now the heart
Of thy abashed oracle, that, for fear,
50   Of some ill it includes, would fain lie hid,
And rise thou with it in thy greater light.

Thunders. BEHEMOTH *rises up with his Spirits.*

Behemoth. Thus, to observe my vow of apparition
In greater light, and explicate thy fate,
I come; and tell thee that, if thou obey
55   The summons that thy mistress next will send thee,
Her hand shall be thy death.
     Bussy.   When will she send?
Behemoth. Soon as I set again, where late I rose.
Bussy. Is the old Friar slain?
Behemoth.   No, and yet lives not.
Bussy. Died he a natural death?
Behemoth.   He did.
Bussy.   Who then
Will my dear mistress send?
60   *Behemoth.*   I must not tell thee.
Bussy. Who lets thee?
Behemoth.   Fate.

35 *into clouds* into obscurity
40 (see p. 105)   42 (see p. 105)   39 (see pp. 104–5)
49 *abashed* hesitant to speak
52 *apparition* double meaning of appearance and ghost
53 *explicate* unfold   61 *lets* prevents

Bussy.   Who are Fate's ministers?
Behemoth. The Guise and Monsieur.
Bussy.   A fit pair of shears
To cut the threads of kings and kingly spirits,
And consorts fit to sound forth harmony
Set to the falls of kingdoms! Shall the hand   65
Of my kind mistress kill me?
Behemoth.   If thou yield
To her next summons. Y'are fair-warned; farewell!
                    Thunders. Exit.

Bussy. I must fare well, however, though I die,
My death consenting with his augury:
Should not my powers obey when she commands,   70
My motion must be rebel to my will,
My will to life. If, when I have obeyed,
Her hand should so reward me, they must arm it,
Bind me and force it; or, I lay my soul
She rather would convert it many times   75
On her own bosom, even to many deaths:
But were there danger of such violence,
I know 'tis far from her intent to send:
And who she should send is as far from thought,
Since he is dead, whose only mean she used.   80
                    [One] knocks.
Who's there? Look to the door, and let him in,
Though politic Monsieur or the violent Guise.

Enter MONTSURRY, *like the* FRIAR *with a letter written
in blood.*

Montsurry. Hail to my worthy son.
Bussy. O lying spirit! Welcome, loved father;
How fares my dearest mistress?
Montsurry.   Well, as ever,   85
Being well as ever thought on by her lord;
Whereof she sends this witness in her hand
And prays, for urgent cause, your speediest presence.
Bussy. What! Writ in blood?   *[Opening the letter.]*
Montsurry.   Ay, 'tis the ink of lovers.
Bussy. Oh, 'tis a sacred witness of her love.   90
So much elixir of her blood as this,

62 (see p. 105)
64 (see p. 105)   69 (see p. 105)   76 (see p. 105)
84 (see p. 105)   91 (see p. 105)

Dropt in the lightest dame, would make her firm
As heat to fire; and, like to all the signs,
Commands the life confined in all my veins;
95 Oh, how it multiplies my blood with spirit,
And makes me apt t'encounter Death and Hell.
But come, kind father, you fetch me to heaven,
And to that end your holy weed was given.   *Exeunt.*

Act V, Scene iii

Enter MONSIEUR *and* GUISE *above.*

Monsieur. Now shall we see that Nature hath no end
In her great works responsive to their worths,
That she, who makes so many eyes and souls
To see and foresee, is stark blind herself;
5 And as illiterate men say Latin prayers
By rote of heart and daily iteration,
In whose hot zeal a man would think they knew
What they ran so away with, and were sure
To have rewards proportioned to their labours,
10 Yet may implore their own confusions
For any thing they know—which often times
It falls out they incur; so Nature lays
A mass of stuff together, and by use,
Or by the mere necessity of matter,
15 Ends such a work, fills it, or leaves it empty
Of strength or virtue, error or clear truth,
Not knowing what she does; but usually
Gives that which we call merit to a man,
And believe should arrive him on huge riches,
20 Honour, and happiness, that effects his ruin;
Right as in ships of war whole lasts of powder
Are laid, men think, to make them last, and guard them,
When a disordered spark that powder taking,

---

93 (see p. 105)   97 (see p. 106)   V, iii (see p. 106)
  2 *responsive* corresponding
  6 *By rote* by heart in a mechanical manner
    iteration repetition
 13 *A mass of stuff* i.e. chaos; *use* mechanical habit
 14 (see p. 106)   17–25 (see p. 106)
 19 *arrive him on* to bring to port
 21 *lasts* units of measurement for ships' cargoes: one or two tons

Blows up with sudden violence and horror
Ships that, kept empty, had sailed long with terror.   25
   Guise. He that observes but like a worldly man
That which doth oft succeed, and by th' events
Values the worth of things, will think it true
That Nature works at random, just with you:
But with as much decorum she may make   30
A thing that from the feet up to the throat
Hath all the wondrous fabric man should have,
And leave it headless, for an absolute man,
As give a whole man valour, virtue, learning,
Without an end more excellent than those   35
On whom she no such worthy part bestows.
   Monsieur. Why, you shall see it here; here will be one
Young, learned, valiant, virtuous, and full-manned;
One on whom Nature spent so rich a hand
That with an ominous eye she wept to see   40
So much consumed her virtuous treasury.
Yet as the winds sing through a hollow tree
And, since it lets them pass through, let it stand;
But a tree solid, since it gives no way
To their wild rages, they rend up by th' root: 45
So this full creature now shall reel and fall
Before the frantic puffs of purblind chance,
That pipes through empty men, and makes them dance.
Not so the sea raves on the Lybian sands,
Tumbling her billows in each others' neck;   50
Not so the surges of the Euxine sea
Near to the frosty pole, where free Boötes
From those dark deep waves turns his radiant team,
Swell, being enraged, even from their inmost drop,
As Fortune swings about the restless state   55
Of virtue, now thrown into all men's hate.

   [*Thunder.*] *The* FRIAR'S *Ghost enters* [*and discovers* TAMYRA]
            wrapped in a canopy.

   Ghost. Revive those stupid thoughts, and sit not thus
Gathering the horrors of your servant's slaughter,
So urged by your hand and so imminent,
Into an idle fancy, but devise   60

27 *th' events* the outcome of actions
29 *just with you* exactly as you do   30 (see p. 106)
38 (see p. 106)   41 *virtuous treasury* i.e. treasury of virtues
49–56 (see p. 106)   56 (see p. 106)   57 (see p. 106)
58–60 (see p. 106)

How to prevent it; watch when he shall rise,
And with a sudden outcry of his murther,
Blow his retreat before he be engaged.
    Tamyra. O father, have my dumb woes waked your death?
65 When will our human griefs be at their height?
Man is a tree that hath no top in cares,
No root in comforts; all his power to live
Is given to no end, but t'have power to grieve.
    Ghost. 'Tis the just curse of our abused creation
70 Which we must suffer here, and scape hereafter.
He hath the great mind that submits to all
He sees inevitable; he the small
That carps at earth and her foundation shaker,
And rather than himself will mend his maker.

        [BUSSY] D'AMBOIS [*appears*] *at the gulf.*

75   *Tamyra.* Away, my love, away! Thou wilt be murthered.
    Bussy. Murthered? I know not what that Hebrew means:
That word had ne'er been named had all been D'Ambois.
Murthered? By heaven, he is my murtherer
That shows me not a murtherer; what such bug
80 Abhorreth not the very sleep of D'Ambois?
Murthered? Who dares give all the room I see
To D'Ambois' reach, or look with any odds
His fight i'th' face, upon whose hand sits death,
Whose sword hath wings, and every feather pierceth?
85 Let in my politic visitants, let them in,
Though entering like so many moving armours.
Fate is more strong than arms, and sly than treason,
And I at all parts buckled in my fate.
Dare they not come?

    Enter MURTHERERS [*at one door*] *with* [*the* FRIAR'S *Ghost*] *at
the other door.*

    Tamyra.   They come.

---

63 (see p. 106)   69 *abused* corrupted   71–4 (see pp. 106–7)
73 *foundation shaker* God
76 *Hebrew* a language one can't understand. *Cf.* 'It's all Greek
   to me.'
79 *bug* bug-bear, imaginary fear
80 *Abhorreth not* is not frightened of
81–2 (see p. 107)   84 (see p. 107)
88 *buckled in* wearing it like a suit of armour

First Murtherer.   Come all at once.
Ghost. Back, coward murtherers, back!
All.   Defend us, heaven!   90
                            Exeunt all but the first.
First Murtherer. Come ye not on?
Bussy.   No, slave, nor goest thou off.
Stand you so firm?—Will it not enter here?
You have a face yet. So! In thy life's flame   *[Kills him.]*
I burn the first rites to my mistress' fame.
    Ghost. Breathe thee, brave son, against the other charge.   95
    Bussy. Oh, is it true then that my sense first told me?
Is my kind father dead?
    Tamyra.   He is, my love.
'Twas the Earl, my husband, in his weed, that brought thee.
    Bussy. That was a speeding sleight, and well resembled.
Where is that angry Earl? My lord, come forth   100
And show your own face in your own affair;
Take not into your noble veins the blood
Of these base villains, nor the light reports
Of blistered tongues for clear and weighty truth,
But me against the world, in pure defence   105
Of your rare lady, to whose spotless name
I stand here as a bulwark, and project
A life to her renown, that ever yet
Hath been untainted, even in envy's eye,
And, where it would protect, a sanctuary.   110
Brave Earl, come forth, and keep your scandal in:
'Tis not our fault if you enforce the spot,
Nor the wreak yours, if you perform it not.

        Enter MONTSURRY, *with all the* MURTHERERS.

    Montsurry. Cowards, a fiend or spirit beat ye off?
They are your own faint spirits that have forged   115
The fearful shadows that your eyes deluded:
The fiend was in you; cast him out then, thus.
        [They fight] D'AMBOIS *hath* MONTSURRY *down.*

    Tamyra. Favour my lord, my love, oh, favour him!
    Bussy. I will not touch him: take your life, my lord,

92 (see p. 107)
95 *Breathe thee* rest in preparation for the next assault
99 (see p. 107)   104 *blistered* perjured
107 *project* offer, push forward   110 (see p. 107)
112 (see p. 107)   113 *wreak* revenge

Comes to terms with own mortality

And be appeased. *Pistols shot within* [BUSSY *is wounded.*]
120   Oh, then the coward Fates
Have maimed themselves, and ever lost their honour.
    Ghost. What have ye done, slaves? Irreligious lord!
    Bussy. Forbear them, father; 'tis enough for me
That Guise and Monsieur, Death and Destiny,
125 Come behind D'Ambois. Is my body then
But penetrable flesh? And must my mind
Follow my blood? Can my divine part add
No aid to th' earthly in extremity?
Then these divines are but for form, not fact:
130 Man is of two sweet courtly friends compact,
A mistress and a servant: let my death
Define life nothing but a courtier's breath.
Nothing is made of nought, of all things made,
Their abstract being a dream but of a shade.
135 I'll not complain to earth yet, but to heaven,
And, like a man, look upwards even in death.
[And if Vespasian thought in majesty
An emperor might die standing, why not I?
                             She offers to help him.
Nay, without help, in which I will exceed him;
140 For he died splinted with his chamber grooms.]
Prop me, true sword, as thou hast ever done!
The equal thought I bear of life and death
Shall make me faint on no side; I am up;
Here like a Roman statue I will stand
145 Till death hath made me marble. Oh, my fame,
Live in despite of murther! Take thy wings
And haste thee where the grey eyed Morn perfumes
Her rosy chariot with Sabaean spices!
Fly, where the Evening from th' Iberian vales
150 Takes on her swarthy shoulders Hecate,
Crowned with a grove of oaks: fly where men feel
The burning axletree, and those that suffer
Beneath the chariot of the snowy Bear:
And tell them all that D'Ambois now is hasting
155 To the eternal dwellers; that a thunder

125 *Come behind* he is shot in the back   129 (see p. 107)
130–1 (see p. 107)   133–4 (see p. 107)   137–40 (see p. 108)
140 *splinted* propped up by   142–3 (see p. 108)
143 (see p. 108)   147–53 (see p. 108)   147–8 (see p. 108)
149 (see p. 108)   150 (see p. 108)   152 (see p. 108)
153 (see p. 108)

Of all their sighs together, for their frailties
Beheld in me, may quit my worthless fall
With a fit volley for my funeral.
 Ghost. Forgive thy murtherers.
 Bussy.   I forgive them all;
And you, my lord, their fautor; for true sign   160
         [*To* MONTSURRY.]
Of which unfeigned remission take my sword;
Take it, and only give it motion,
And it shall find the way to victory
By his own brightness, and th' inherent valour
My fight hath stilled into't with charms of spirit. 165
And let me pray you that my weighty blood,
Laid in one scale of your impartial spleen,
May sway the forfeit of my worthy love
Weighed in the other; and be reconciled *noble*
With all forgiveness to your matchless wife.   170
 Tamyra. Forgive thou me, dear servant, and this hand
That led thy life to this unworthy end;
Forgive it, for the blood with which 'tis stained,
In which I writ the summons of thy death—
The forced summons—by this bleeding wound, 175
By this here in my bosom, and by this
That makes me hold up both my hands imbrued
For thy dear pardon.
 Bussy.   Oh, my heart is broken!
Fate nor these murtherers, Monsieur nor the Guise,
Have any glory in my death, but this,   180
This killing spectacle, this prodigy:
My sun is turned to blood 'gainst whose red beams
Pindus and Ossa, hid in endless snow,
Laid on my heart and liver, from their veins
Melt like two hungry torrents, eating rocks, 185
Into the ocean of all human life,
And make it bitter, only with my blood.
Oh, frail condition of strength, valour, virtue,
In me, like warning fire upon the top
Of some steep beacon, on a steeper hill,   190
Made to express it: like a falling star
Silently glanced, that like a thunderbolt

155–8 (see p. 108) 157 *quit.* requite 160 *fautor* abettor
161 (see p. 108)   165 (see pp. 108–9) 167 (see p. 109)
177 *imbrued* stained 182–7 (see pp. 109–10) 191 (see p. 110)

Looked to have stuck and shook the firmament.

Dies.

Ghost. Son of the earth, whom my unrested soul,
[*To* MONTSURRY]
195 Rues t'have begotten in the faith of heaven,
Since thy revengeful spirit hath rejected
The charity it commands, and the remission,
To serve and worship the blind rage of blood,
Assay to gratulate and pacify
200 The soul fled from this worthy by performing
The Christian reconcilement he besought
Betwixt thee and thy lady; let her wounds
Manlessly digged in her, be eased and cured
With balm of thine own tears; or be assured
205 Never to rest free from my haunt and horror.
    Montsurry. See how she merits this; still sitting by,
And mourning his fall more than her own fault!
    Ghost. Remove, dear daughter, and content thy husband;
So piety wills thee, and thy servant's peace.
210   *Tamyra.* O wretched piety, that art so distract
In thine own constancy, and in thy right
Must be unrighteous: if I right my friend
I wrong my husband; if his wrong I shun,
The duty of my friend I leave undone:
215 Ill plays on both sides; here and there, it riseth;
No place, no good, so good, but ill compriseth;
My soul more scruple breeds than my blood, sin;
Virtue imposeth more than any stepdame:
Oh, had I never married but for form,
220 Never vowed faith but purposed to deceive,
Never made conscience of any sin,
But cloaked it privately and made it common;
Nor never honoured been in blood or mind;
Happy had I been then, as others are
225 Of the like licence; I had then been honoured;
Lived without envy; custom had benumbed
All sense of scruple and all note of frailty;
My fame had been untouched, my heart unbroken:

194 (see p. 110)
199 *Assay* attempt *gratulate* appease, recompense
203 *Manlessly* in an unmanly, inhuman way
209 *thy servant's peace* i.e. Bussy's   210 (see p. 110)
221 *made conscience* made a matter of conscience
223–5 (see p. 110)

But, shunning all, I strike on all offence;
O husband! Dear friend! O my conscience!   *hard &*   230
        cold
   Montsurry. I must not yield to pity nor to love
So servile and so traitorous: cease, my blood,
To wrestle with my honour, fame, and judgment:
Away, forsake my house, forbear complaints
Where thou hast bred them: here [are] all things full   235
Of their own shame and sorrow; leave my house.
   Tamyra. Sweet lord, forgive me, and I will be gone,
And till these wounds, that never balm shall close
Till death hath entered at them—so I love them,
Being opened by your hands—by death be cured,   240
I never more will grieve you with my sight,
Never endure that any roof shall part
Mine eyes and heaven; but to the open deserts,
Like to hunted tigers I will fly,
Eating my heart, shunning the steps of men,   245
And look on no side till I be arrived.
   Montsurry. I do forgive thee, and upon my knees,
With hands held up to heaven, wish that mine honour
Would suffer reconcilement to my love;
But since it will not, honour, never serve   250
My love with flourishing object, till it sterve!
And as this taper, though it upwards look,
Downwards must needs consume, so let our love!
As, having lost his honey, the sweet taste
Runs into savour, and will needs retain   255
A spice of his first parents, till, like life,
It sees and dies; so let our love! And lastly,
As when the flame is suffered to look up,
It keeps his lustre, but, being thus turned down,
His natural course of useful light inverted,   260
His own stuff puts it out, so let our love!
Now turn from me, as here I turn from thee,
And may both points of heaven's straight axletree
Conjoin in one, before thyself and me.

        Exeunt [MONTSURRY *and* TAMYRA] *severally.*

   Ghost. My terrors are struck inward, and no more   265

---

231 In B, Guise and Montsurry exit with a short speech
235 Dilke added 'are', not in A or B
246 *arrived* at my port, i.e. die
251 *sterve* die   252–61 (see p. 110–11)   254 (see p. 111)
257 (see p. 111)   261–2 (see pp. 111)

My penance will allow they shall enforce
Earthly afflictions but upon myself.
Farewell, brave relicts of a complete man;
Look up and see thy spirit made a star;
270   Join flames with Hercules, and when thou settest
Thy radiant forehead in the firmament,
Make the vast continent, cracked with thy receipt,
Spread to a world of fire, and th'aged sky
Cheer with new sparks of old humanity.   *Exit.*

EPILOGUE

WITH many hands you have seen D'Ambois slain,
Yet by your grace he may revive again,
And every day grow stronger in his skill
To please, as we presume he is in will.
5   The best deserving actors of the time
Had their ascents; and by degrees did climb
To their full height, a place to study due.
To make him tread in their path lies in you;
He'll not forget his makers, but still prove
10   His thankfulness, as you increase your love.

Finis

268–74 (see p. 111)   268 (see pp. 111–12)   269–70 (see p. 112)
271 (see p. 112)   272 (see p. 112)

CRITICAL NOTES

7   I.i, 1–80. The first eighty lines are packed with echoes of Plutarch's *Moralia*. *Cf*. lines 6–17 and *To an uneducated Ruler* for Chapman's fidelity to his source:
'But most kings and rulers are so foolish as to act like unskilful sculptors, who think their colossal figures look large and imposing if they are modelled with their feet far apart, their muscles tense, and their mouths wide open. For these rulers seem by heaviness of voice, harshness of expression, truculence of manner, and unsociability in their way of living to be imitating the dignity and majesty of the princely station, although in fact they are not at all different from colossal statues which have a heroic and godlike form on the outside, but inside are full of clay, stone, and lead'. (Loeb. vol. X. F.779.)
For detailed analysis, see Brooke, Appendix B(f); F.L. Schoell, *Études sur l'Humanisme continental en Angleterre à la Fin de la Renaissance* Paris, 1926, pp. 197–9; A. S. Ferguson, 'The Plays of George Chapman', *Modern Language Review XIII*, 1918, pp. 2–5.

7   I.i, 10. *tympanous statists*. A tympany was a tumour or swelling, sometimes used metaphorically, as of pride. Statist: politician. *Cf*. 'Timpanies of state.' (To Harriot accompanying *Achilles' Shield*, line 78.)

7   I.i, 19. *summed with all his substance*. When all his achievements and material possessions are added up together.

8   I.i, 34. *numerous state*. Containing many units; by its suggestion of number leading to 'cipher'—nought—in the next line. 'The king is the unit giving significance to the row of noughts that follow.' (Ferguson, p. 5.)

8   I.i, 39–40. *tracts . . . facts*. No tracks or examples for poor men to follow as a precedent for their deeds.

8   I.i, 59. *the gross Sicilian gourmandist*. Gnatho. Chapman uses the same image in his *Preface to the Reader* to *Homer's Iliads*. ed. Nicoll, p. 18.

9   I.i, 81. *by which we live*. By which our fame is perpetuated and by which we all profit.

9   I.i, 86–7. *brake*. A frame or vice with which to hold things steady, hence, to keep a set face.

9   I.i, 89. *dame-school mistresses*. A and B read 'Dames
     Schoolmistresses'; Parrott, 'dame schoolmistresses'. A
     dame-school was a school for young children, but Chapman
     is perhaps suggesting a characteristic double meaning, the
     mistress of a school for dames, a bawd. *Cf.* IV.i. 50. for
     the idea in reverse—'The school of modesty not to learn
     learns dames.' Chapman uses 'Dame' constantly to
     imply woman's frailty—e.g. 'Weak dames' (III.i, 47). In
     this case the riddle is presumably the kind of bawdy
     riddle such as Pero produces at III.ii. 250. The implica-
     tions of deceit in the image of the magic mirror ('that
     enchanted glass'), and the cheating game of fast and loose
     (*Cf. Antony and Cleopatra*, IV.x, 41)—are maintained
     in the double meaning of 'shift' meaning both sophistry
     and a woman's smock.

9   I.i, 100. *believe backwards*. Possibly a reference to the prac-
     tices of Black Magic and the Black Mass which involved
     inversion of the liturgy. (Brooke.)

10   I.i, 102. *t'unfold their art*. Hearing sermons preached
     against villainy, learn to commit it so as to know how it is
     done.

10   I.i, 109. *brave barks*. A typical pun on barque; the 'tall
     ships' of I.i, 22 as well as rich clothes and outer coverings.

10   I.i, 122–6. *Like to disparking . . . seed-land*. I have included
     these lines although they were added in B. A has 'but he's
     no husband here; a smooth plain ground . . .' Chapman
     uses the metaphor of ploughing in connection with poli-
     ticians again at IV.ii, 171; his conception of Learning as
     the enemy of Policy is considered in the Introduction
     (p. xvi). Bussy insists that he is both a scholar and a poet
     (I.i, 187), the two being for Chapman inseparable.
     Ferguson (p. 5) finds a further reference to the *Hercules
     Oetaeus* in the passage, an additional reason for thinking
     it by Chapman.

10   I.i, 122. *disparking*. A reference to a common complaint of
     the period, that the nobility are being forced to sell their
     land.

10   I.i, 124. *unsweating thrift*. A reflection of the Elizabethan
     mistrust of making money without working for it,
     especially strong in an age of economic speculation. *Cf.* 'I
     wound no earth with ploughshares.' (*Volpone* I.i, 34);
     also *The Faerie Queene* Bk. II. Canto III, 40–41.

10   I.i, 124. *policy . . . politic*. Chapman, like Shakespeare,
     always uses the term in a strongly derogatory sense:
     Machiavellian.

11   I.i, 144–Chapman makes Maffé a ridiculous parody of
      Monsieur, his master, both in his clumsy attempts at
      'policy' (line 206) and in his unconscious use of double
      entendre—'ass . . . ears' (202), 'Husband . . . standing'
      (210). Monsieur's speeches are habitually full of in-
      nuendo.

11   I.i, 144. *Humour*. The name for the four chief fluids of the
      body (blood, phlegm, choler, melancholy), which con-
      ditioned the health, character and moods. Used also to
      describe the characteristic mood or temperament associ-
      ated with a particular humour.

12   I.i, 193. *fair great noses*. Anjou was noted for his large and
      deformed nose. (Parrott.)

13   I.i, 208. *his wooden dagger*. The property of the Vice in the
      old Morality plays and Interludes, and sometimes carried
      by the Elizabethan jester for which Maffé mistakes
      Bussy. (Boas.)

14   I.ii, 12. *their old Queen*. An allusion not likely to be made
      while Elizabeth was alive, hence a pointer to the date of
      the play, as post 1603.

14   I.ii, 21. *informed*. Given form, in the Platonic sense. The
      court derives its essential quality from the queen, in
      contrast to the 'deformity' (line 30) of the French court.

14   I.ii, 22. *The world is not contracted in a man*. A reference to
      the common Mediæval and Renaissance conception of
      man as the microcosm of the whole world.

14   I.ii, 37–48. The travelled Englishman's affectation of the
      fashions of other countries is a stock theme of Elizabethan
      satire. *Cf. The Merchant of Venice*, I.ii, 78–.

15   I.ii, 53. There is fine irony in the entry of Bussy in his new
      suit immediately after Henry's comments on the vanity
      of fine clothes.

15   I.ii, 64. Bussy's simple statement about wooing virtue is
      perverted by Monsieur in a typical manner into an
      image of prostitution. 'Give her those rites'—i.e. money
      and clothes; hence, 'Th'art mine.'

15   I.ii, 70. *too many/ To be in council*. Perhaps referring to the
      fact that James increased the size of the Privy Council on
      his accession, by the inclusion of a number of Scots. For
      further jibes at James' promotion of his compatriots, see
      line 110, 'some knight of the new edition', and line 154,
      'some new denizened lord', newly naturalized, from
      Scotland. The new Scottish Knights were a common
      topic for satire.

16   I.ii, 80. *prick-song*. Music sung from notes written down or 'pricked' out. Here involving a low pun, as in 'leap-year' (line 77).

16   I.ii, 82. *rotten before he be ripe*. A common saying derived from the nature of the medlar and carrying implications of sex and prostitution. *Cf. The Atheist's Tragedy*, IV.i, 2. In this case, it is a sneer at Bussy's over-eagerness.

16   I.ii, 90. *courtship*. The behaviour proper to courtiers; here used with reference to the formalized code of behaviour between the sexes, descended from the mediaeval Courts of love and comprising the compliment, chases of wit, etc. recommended in the Courtesy books of the period and exemplified in the exchanges of *Love's Labour's Lost*, for example.

16   I.ii, 98. *Accius Naevius*. The Roman augur who at the command of Tarquin cut through a whetstone with a razor. (Parrott.)

16   I.ii, 102. *y'ave cut too many throats already*. A reference to the Guise's share in the massacre of the Protestants on St. Bartholomew's day, 1572.

17   I.ii, 116. *the knight's ward*. A part reserved for people of quality in the Counter, a London prison where debtors were confined. Here an allusion to Bussy's former poverty.

17   I.ii, 142. *The divers frames*. The land shapes and sea bed which frame and control the movement of the sea.

17   I.ii, 147. *the mate*. Referring to the game of chess in progress and also, ironically, to the Guise's inability to stop Bussy from courting his Duchess.

17   I.ii, 149. *here's a lion . . . cock*. It was a popular superstition that lions were afraid of the crowing of a cock. Browne discusses the matter in *Pseudodoxia*, Bk. III, XXVII, 7.

18   I.ii, 152. *jig*. Light entertainment at the end of a play or in between the acts.

18   I.ii, 161–2. *the ass . . . the lion's case*. An allusion to Aesop's fable of the ass in the lion's skin.

19   I.ii, 190–1. *descants . . . ground*. The 'ground' is the tune and the 'descant' the melodious accompaniment sung or played around it. In this case, the 'ground' is Bussy's new suit, and the 'descant' the comments with which Barrisor and his friends embroider it; but Bussy is also referring contemptuously to 'this ground', i.e. the Royal Presence Chamber where they can make such insulting remarks in safety.

19   I.ii, 209. *out of this privilege.* Out of the Court limits within
      which there were especially heavy penalties for braw-
      ling. (Parrott.)

19   II.i, Stage Directions: A has: Henry, Guise, Beaumond,
      Nuntius, although the messenger does not in fact enter
      until line 24. B has: Henry, Guise, Montsurry and
      attendants, omitting Beaumond although attributing the
      short speech, lines 105–6, to him. Presumably the
      revisor was economizing on characters but forgot to
      alter the name in the text. Parrott retains Beaumond;
      Boas re-assigns the speech to Montsurry.

20   II.i, 24 s.d. *Enter Nuntius.* The classical messenger of Greek
      tragedy who came to Elizabethan drama via Seneca. He
      is in keeping with Chapman's conception of his play as a
      tragedy and speaks in the grand heroic style with Homeric
      allusions, latinized syntax and set similes.

20   II.i, 35. Chapman may have got the idea for this three-a-
      side duel from one fought in 1578 between three followers
      of Henry III and three of the Guise's supporters. Bussy
      did not take part.

20–1 II.i, 39–47. *All which . . . from other.* The punctuation of
      this passage is difficult. A has a colon after 'stood ranked',
      and a comma after 'Like forms of life and death', so that
      'each took from other' is related back directly to the
      image of the mirror. B replaces the colon after 'contribu-
      torie wood' by a comma, and removes the comma after
      'like forms of life and death', making the whole passage
      entirely fluid. I have kept as near to A as possible. 'All
      which arrived' (39) is a participle clause—'When all had
      arrived.' 'Like bonfires' (44) is in apposition—'Similar
      bonfires.' 'Like forms of life and death' (47) is the object
      of 'shewed.'

21   II.i, 44. *bonfires of contributory wood.* Presumably fires that
      kindle each other and contribute to the total fire.

21   II.i, 54. *As Hector.* From Homer's *Iliads*, III, 83—when
      Paris offered to settle the war in single combat with
      Menelaus, and Hector 'rusht betwixt the fighting hoasts
      and made the Troyans cease/By holding up in midst his
      lance.'

21   II.i, 60. *Ripped up the quarrel.* Suggested by the fact that
      Barrisor separated the two sides with his rapier. The
      O.E.D. also gives 'to open up, to bring into discussion'.

21   II.i, 63. *conclude.* Bring to an end the dangers in which the
      others stood by settling the matter in single combat.

21 II.i, 78–80. *Cf.* the wounds of angels in *Paradise Lost*, VI, 328–50.

22 II.i, 84–7. Three times Bussy tries to pluck out his sword and each time draws thrusts from Barrisor which he (Bussy) is quick enough to escape.

22 II.i, 89. *his yet undaunted foe.* Barrisor who, made more horrid with his wound, forces Bussy to give ground.

22 II.i, 94. *Arden.* Always the forest of Romance in Elizabethan literature. (Parrott.) The long set simile is modelled on *Aeneid*, II, 626–32.

22 II.i, 104. *Navarre.* Later Henry IV of France who was at the height of his military fame at the time the play was written, long after the death of Bussy.

22 II.i, 108. *Thy felt report calls on.* Your account which has moved us calls for more.

22 II.i, 110. *two opposite fumes.* The exhalations which, when trapped in a cloud, cause thunder by their breaking out. See Aristotle, *Meteorologica*, II.ix, and Introduction (pp. xxvi–vii).

22 II.i, 118. *Armenia.* Referred to as the haunt of wild animals in *Hercules-Oetaeus*, line 241.

23 II.i, 119–23. *the treasure of his brow.* Unicorn's horn was commonly believed to be an antidote against poisons and to have magical properties in charms. See Browne's discussion of its 'antidotal efficiency' in *Pseudodoxia*, Bk. III, xxiii. Hunters caught unicorns by standing against a tree and side stepping so that the beast impaled itself when it charged. *Cf. The Faerie Queene*, II.v, 10.

23 II.i, 130. *honour at the view.* A hunting term: 'press hard after honour, like hounds that have caught sight of the chase.' (Parrott.)

23 II.i, 135. *freckled.* As in B. A has 'feebled'. *Cf. The Revenge of Bussy*, I.i, 117–18: 'the blood/She so much thirsts for, freckling hands and face.'

23 II.i, 141–8. A difficult passage. Monsieur's 'policy' makes him wrap up his plea in language designed at once to flatter the king and blunt the crudity of his request. The meaning would seem to be 'If ever Nature can be truly herself when the natural duties of King to subject (greatness) come into conflict with the natural duties of brother to brother (virtue) now reconcile these two duties, or raise both of them to truly kingly heights by performing an act of supreme brotherly love (i.e. pardoning a murderer) which at the same time enhances your kingly greatness since only a king could perform it.'

For a fuller analysis of the passage, see Ferguson, p. 6.

23–4 II.i, 150–9. Monsieur defends duelling on the grounds of Equity, that it is a species ('spice') of justice which rights those offences outside ('past') the law. He contrasts the natural law of reputation with the 'positive law' of the legal code, and argues that where the latter does not lay down beforehand ('prefix') adequate redress, a free man may supply the deficiency himself. Henry counters that every man who thinks himself wronged, whether justly or not ('or in wrong or right') will be tempted to take the law into his own hands.

24   II.i, 163–4. Both A and B and all editors have a semi-colon after 'butchers' and print line 164 as a question: 'Should this fact, though of justice, be forgiven?' The quartos use question marks very loosely, however, and the line seems to me to be no question but a rounding off of the whole speech—'all men would think themselves law-menders though mere butchers, if this deed, even though just in itself, should be forgiven.' Monsieur's 'Oh, no' in the next line is not an answer to a question but a counter to the King's whole argument. Presumably the compositor mistook the two lines for question and answer.

24   II.i, 166. *full men.* In Chapman's use of the term, a virtuous, learned, complete man. *Cf.* V.iii, 46, the contrast between 'this full creature' and the 'empty men.' B's emendation to 'whole man' weakens the meaning.

24   II.i, 175. *th' under value.* The physical life of his enemy which is inferior to 'fame's dear life' and is justly forfeited for the wrong it did.

24   II.i, 179. *murther men alive.* Worthier to survive than the many who murder men's honour though leaving their victims physically alive.

24–5 II.i, 190–. The grace for which Bussy kneels a second time is not the pardon from 'merited death' which has already been granted, since he does not accept that he has committed any crime. He is demanding the right to be 'king myself' and above the law where the law fails to do justice. Chapman always insists that the truly virtuous man needs no law. See Henry's reference to 'man in his native noblesse' (III.ii, 91); also *Byron's Conspiracy*, III.iii, 141, and *The Gentleman Usher*, (V.iv, 56–62).

25   II.i, 211. *I have obtained a kingdom.* A fine piece of irony. Under the assertion of friendship, Monsieur hints at his ultimate purpose in rescuing Bussy—to kill the King.

25   II.ii, There is extensive re-writing in the later version at this point. B omits Monsieur's final couplet at the end of II.i, but adds seven lines of unnecessary soliloquy by Bussy in which he confesses his feigned love for the Duchess and his real love for Tamyra. The first fifty lines of II.ii in A are, however, omitted, including the important speech of Tamyra (II.ii, 34–49) declaring her uncontrollable passion. II.ii in B begins at line 50 with the entry of Monsieur.

25   II.ii, 3. *still borne.* Continue to be tolerated if they spring from greatness. Brooke suggests 'still-born.' Possibly both senses are present.

26   II.ii, 15. *project.* Brooke suggests 'forward-thrusting', impudent. Jacquot sees a punning connection with the alchemical term, projection, the turning of base metals to gold; hence 'test' in the next line. Tamyra implies that Bussy in his new clothes is an impostor, common metal masquerading as gold.

26   II.ii, 34. This is the theory of the cause of earthquakes outlined by Aristotle in *Meteorologica*, II.viii. They spring from the imprisonment of exhalations in the earth. 'her' (36, 37) refers to the earth; 'his' (39) to the fume.

27   II.ii, 41. *All bars.* All impediments are made the means to fulfillment. The 'holy man' who has always 'counselled for my soul' but is now to be made 'an agent for my blood' is a case in point.

27   II.ii, 49. *blood.* The Humour especially associated with sexual passion. It should be controlled by soul but has reversed the proper hierarchy. See Introduction and reference to *Hymnus in Cynthiam* (p. xviii).

27   II.ii, 51. The whole dialogue between Monsieur and Tamyra is full of sexual innuendo.

28   II.ii, 84. *maritorious.* Constantly invoking and referring to one's husband, uxorious. *meritorious.* As well as the normal sense, the O.E.D. gives 'that earns money by prostitution.'

28   II.ii, 94–5. *So ill prepared* 'with such evil conditions attached to it that I can take a poison disguised beneath the medicine as cheaply as the medicine itself.' Pearls were ground up and used in medicinal potions.

29   II.ii, 115. *Matter of death.* Some husbands would challenge Monsieur to a duel.

29   II.ii, 120–3. *their prerogatives . . . essence.* 'Just as princes grant pardons and withdraw them as soon as parliament stops sitting, so their apparent conformity to the law is

nullified by the use of the Royal Prerogative to break it—
they cancel each other out. The outward appearance of
conformity is all they are concerned with.'

29   II.ii, 136–43. The passage is full of the hackneyed conceits
of the love poetry of the period—lovers compared to the
sun, exchanging souls, dying of absence, etc. Tamyra
would die as her soul departs with her husband, if he did
not give her his own in exchange. *Cf.* Sidney: 'My true
love hath my heart and I have his.' The sudden burst of
conventional conceits in the passage draws attention to
Tamyra's hypocrisy, as again on Montsurry's return the
next morning. (III.i, 71–4.)

30   II.ii, 146. I have included as authentic this line added in
B, because the paradoxical quality of 'dark light' fits in
well with that of the still centre of the turning world
(line 165), and the conjunction of opposites is reminiscent
of Chapman's *Hymnus in Noctem.* The image leads on to
that of the waning moon.

30   II.ii, 147–9. 'As our love wanes we supply its place with a
growing dissimulation in which even the most innocent
become fully experienced.' The image of the moon growing to the full introduces that of the maid becoming a
mother and is picked up ironically in, 'Go, maid, to bed;'
(line 153). 'services' (155) usually implies the services of
a lover.

30   II.ii, 152. *most vice shows most divine.* The greater the vice,
the greater the show of virtue. Tamyra exemplifies this
when she borrows Pero's book, 'Not, like yourself, for
form.' (line 154), i.e. not just to give the appearance of
reading while in fact listening in to the conversation.

30   II.ii, 161. *ominous secureness.* Brooke points out that
'ominous' could have the sense of good as well as bad:
hence 'omens of security, freedom from anxiety.' In the
context of Tamyra's speech it must also carry some of its
normal connotations and imply a false sense of security.

30   II.ii, 165. *the Centre.* The hypothetical 'still point of the
turning world' which is also the centre of the revolving
spheres of the Ptolemaic system.

30   II.ii, 165–6. *the violent wheels.* The wheels of clocks, and
Fortune's rolling restless wheel.

30   II.ii, 167. *The Maker's treasury.* The created universe
through which the Creator shows forth himself in all his
riches.

30   II.ii, 179. An ambiguous passage. In her conflict between
fear and desire, Tamyra wishes simultaneously to escape

from her love for Bussy and to cast off her old self so that
she may begin anew with him.

31   II.ii, 193. *colour*. The 'colours' of rhetoric were the tech-
niques of presenting a matter in the most persuasive way.
In this case, the 'colour' is the innocent excuse with
which Bussy is to cover his real reason for being there.

31   II.ii, 195. *the first orb move*. The Primum Mobile, i.e. the
outermost sphere of the Ptolemaic system which set in
motion the other nine spheres within it.

31   II.ii, 196. *set*. Presumably unmoving, still, until given
motion by Bussy. 'Cunning', since needing such Machia-
vellian methods to make it begin turning. The friar's
image of a world set turning is especially ironical after
Tamyra's wish for all the wheels of time and fortune to
stand still. (II.ii, 165).

31   II.ii, 199. The extremely tortuous syntax of the friar's
speech is appropriate to the indirect methods he is
advocating. The holy friar becomes a politician like
Monsieur—'For the direct is crooked.' *Cf.* Polonius'
windlasses and assays of bias.

32   II.ii, 228–9. *If not dissemble . . . satisfied*. 'If she is not
given opportunity to dissemble or show petulence, she is
not satisfied even if she gains her wish.' (Boas.)

32   II.ii, 235–7. The four humours were concocted by the
liver from food and thence carried to the appropriate
parts of the body by the blood. They must be indulged
because they dictate the whole psychological make-up
of the person concerned.

33   II.ii, 264. Although troubled by the thought of God's all-
seeing eye, Tamyra is not able to press the point in case it
breeds scruples in Bussy. Her conclusion is not that they
should avoid sin but that they should be careful (curious)
to avoid being discovered. The speech embodies Tamyra's
inner conflict in which her religious scruples are challenged and defeated by her passion.

34   III.i, 9–28. There is a full analysis of Tamyra's speech and
Bussy's reply to her fears by Ferguson, pp. 7–8.

34   III.i, 24. *When they hold no proportion*. When there is really
no resemblance.

34   III.i, 25–7. *monster . . . cloth*. Policy paints a distorted
picture of sin, just as the owner of a freak show at a fair
has a picture outside making his exhibits look more
monstrous than they are in reality.

34   III.i, 31–2. *our three powers*. Besides his own specifically

'rational' soul, man also had the 'sensible' soul of animals and the 'vegetable' soul of plants, the three being associated with the brain, heart and liver respectively. For the symbolism of three friends as one, see *The Faerie Queene*, Book IV. III and the three brothers, Priamond, Diamond and Triamond.

35   III.i, 42. *It rests*. The secret remains as inviolable as if . . . (Boas.)

35   III.i, 42. B adds seventeen lines of dialogue here between Tamyra, Bussy and the friar who returns to conduct Bussy away. The passage contains an amusing exhibition of hypocrisy on the part of Tamyra but it also simplifies and cheapens her character after the subtle picture already given of the real conflict between her conscience and her passion. There is a good ironic touch at the end when she gives Bussy a chain of pearl. *Cf.* Monsieur's remark, II.ii, 98.

35   III.i, 44–6. As statesmen make poor men commit crimes as a means of achieving the just ends at which their policy is aimed, the end justifies the means.

35   III.i, 50. *our still-undone labours*. Our efforts to be virtuous, constantly begun again and as constantly overthrown. Tamyra's passion is reflected in the sexual overtones of her speech.

35   III.i, 50–2. Nature dictates the use we make of our powers as the plumb-line sets the line to which the stones are laid in building a wall, not vice versa. The image is taken from Plutarch's *Moralia*.

35   III.i, 57. *Oft-times inverts*. The metaphor is of a clock finger turning the wrong way.

35   III.i, 61–3. Even the sun has to wait for the mists to clear which his own heat has drawn up, before he can shine on us.

36   III.i, 98. *Fortune's proud mushroom*. An ironical piece of double entendre especially after Montsurry's praise of the Friar two lines before.

36   III.i, 99. *Atlas*. Brother of Prometheus who, with the Titans, made war upon Jove and was condemned to bear the weight of the heavens.

37   III.ii, 4. *check at nothing*. To check was a hawking term meaning to forsake the quarry for baser game—in this case, for nothing at all. B clarifies the meaning by substituting 'sparrows' for 'nothing.'

37   III.ii, 5. *And bear my thunder*. Jove's eagle bore thunder

beneath its wings. See *Eugenia* lines 742–5 and Chapman's gloss on the passage.

37   III.ii, 9–14. Truth is chained up as the devil is chained in Hell; only flattery goes free.

37   III.ii, 13. *boots of hay-ropes*. Bands of hay were sometimes wrapped round the legs to serve instead of boots or protect the hose. (Boas.) The image of the flatterer so protected by the 'soothed guts' of kings—the lower nature, associated with liver and intestines, and won over by Flattery—is an ugly picture of life at court.

37   III.ii, 18. *red-haired man*. Judas in tapestries was popularly represented as having red-hair, and stage jews, such as Shylock, traditionally wore red wigs.

37   III.ii, 22. *lucern*. Normally a lynx, though the O.E.D. gives 'a kind of hunting dog', quoting as its authority Chapman's *Iliads*, XI, 417; 'As when a den of bloodie Lucerns cling/About a goodly palmed Hart hurt with a hunter's bow.' Here, as in *Bussy*, Chapman could simply mean a beast of prey.

38   III.ii, 29. *suffering king*. The King who allows it and also suffers under it.

38   III.ii, 31–6. This complex series of images gives a vivid and amusing picture of the precarious shifts to which 'Greatness' is driven in its endeavour to maintain its state and balance while at the same time manoeuvring to adapt itself to changing circumstances. The image is of woodmongers carrying a great pile of timber balanced with difficulty on a jolting cart. The great man and his underlings are built up into a great hierarchy (graduate) which must be moved on a cart whose wheels (turning props) are those of 'Protean law'. Proteus was the old man of the sea who, in the Odyssey (Book IV), changed his shape to avoid questioning by Menelaus. *Cf. The Faerie Queene* III.viii, 40, where he is the symbol of change. These 'Protean' wheels, therefore, suggest the wheel of Fortune. The great man and his train must effect this difficult journey and at the same time 'Keep all upright'—i.e. keep the whole structure standing and perhaps, too, keep within the law. Ferguson suggests that lines 32–3, 'Raising each other', contain a reference to the giants piling up mountains in order to reach heaven. (p. 10.)

38   III.ii, 35. *his own counsel keeping*. Keeping the matter secret but also, as Parrott suggests, keeping his own private lawyer, like Sir Giles Overreach in *A New Way to Pay Old Debts*. 'Convey' in the previous line—a legal

term often associated with sharp practices—supports this interpretation. *Cf.* III.ii, 208.

38   III.ii, 37. *the vulture.* Either the vulture with which Jove afflicted Prometheus or that which tortured Tityus. (*Aeneid*, VI.)

38   III.ii, 44. *superfluous cures.* A reference to pluralist clergymen. (Parrott.)

39   III.ii, 69. *popular purple.* Purple was the imperial colour. Guise wore it in Paris to impress the populace. (Boas.)

39   III.ii, 76. *nobly born.* A has 'noblie,' B 'nobly'. Boas and Parrott emend to 'noblier.' The emendation follows from the comparatives of the previous lines—better, more, greater—but the change is unnecessary. If Bussy is a bastard he is not noble in the sense in which Monsieur and the Guise use the word, and they tell him so. Bussy denies, however, that nobility has anything to do with noble birth; it springs from inner merit. Hence he is noble and the Guise is not.

39   III.ii, 79. *Cardinal of Ambois.* Archbishop of Rouen, Bussy's great-uncle who died in 1510.

39   III.ii, 84. *great in faction.* In the number of his supporters, the size of his party, with an underlying suggestion of sedition.

39   III.ii, 86. *That men's souls are without them.* That men's greatness lies in outward trappings, the 'outward patches of our frailty/Riches and honour' that take the place of inner merit.

40   III.ii, 108. *the Hermean rod.* Hermes' caduceus bearing the image of two serpents twined. An emblem of peace.

40   III.ii, 110. *supporters.* A heraldic term for the figures holding up or standing beside the shield, as well as the normal meaning of the word.

41   III.ii, 131. B has a brief sequence here giving Tamyra, the Duchess and Montsurry who have been silent throughout the scene a chance to speak, and leading on to Monsieur's intrigue in the next sequence.

41   III.ii, 136–9. A reference to the giant Typhon, in one account the son of Juno alone, who challenged Jove. He was struck down by 'Jove's great ordnance'—his thunderbolt—and buried under Aetna.

41   III.ii, 146. *scapes to please advantage.* Commit escapades which give their enemies an advantage over them.

(Brooke)

41   III.ii, 147–8. *women . . . candles.* Tilley quotes a proverb: 'He that worst may must hold the candle.' (p. 78.C.40.)

(M. P. Tilley, *A Dictionary of the Proverbs in England in the Sixteenth and Seventeenth Centuries.*) This normally means that the weakest goes to the wall, but Monsieur uses it to mean that the weak person can still throw light on affairs. He also loads it with an obscene suggestion in keeping with the rest of the speech.

41   III.ii, 152–6. The revised version in B is neater and the scansion more regular. Brooke accepts it, but there seems to me nothing in it especially characteristic of Chapman and I therefore retain A.

41   III.ii, 156. *To beat his vault.* Turberville's *Booke of Hunting* (Tudor and Stuart Library), Chap. 17 on the rut and vault of hartes, mentions both beating and vaulting, though not coupled together as in Chapman. 'The old hartes go sooner to vault' and when the young harts come near they 'beate and dryve them away' (p. 44). Elsewhere harts fighting for the female 'beginne to vault and to scrape the ground' (p. 45). Possibly Chapman's phrase means to clear a space and remove all opposition before going to the rut.

42   III.ii, 170. *engaged.* Caught, with the suggestion of being engaged in an encounter in love's war.

42   III.ii, 194. *at a banquet.* Brooke suggests that the term implies sexual intercourse, and quotes the O.E.D. 'To furnyse a bancat/In Venus chalmer' (Dunbar) as well as Chapman's own Ovid's *Banquet of Sense.* Monsieur's advice that Bussy should bring light to Fortune's banquet (I.i, 62) has had ironic results. B replaces the phrase with the more literal 'reading a letter.'

42–3   III.ii, 199–201. A reads '. . . thy Lady his dam: infinite regions. . . .' B, which I follow, seems less likely to be the result of deliberate revision than of the inclusion of lines accidentally omitted by the compositor of A.

43   III.ii, 213. *let's favour our apprehensions.* Let's give our imaginations a rest by not thinking about it.

43   III.ii, 224–5. *your Countess.* A has 'your Lady, or the Countess Beaupre', but Beaupré was not a countess. I follow Brooke in assuming that the titles were transposed.

43   III.ii, 229. *dry palm.* A sign of chastity, as a moist one was a sign of amorousness. *Cf. Othello,* III.iv, 36.

43   III.ii, 230. *Sh'as a liver.* For the link between the liver and love, see *Love's Labour's Lost,* IV.iii, 74, 'The liver vein.'

44   III.ii, 250–5. Pero's riddle concerns maidenhead. 'In' is perhaps a verb, to enter in, distend.

44   III.ii, 270. *winter plum.* Fruit ripening very late, hence the

opposite of a medlar: applied to someone over virginal. Monsieur's remark in the next line about the 'fruit of our inquisition . . . budding' is a cynical allusion to Tamyra whom he now places in the same category as the waiting women.

45 III.ii, 291. *Scylla and Charybdis*. The rock and the whirl-pool between which Odysseus had to steer. Chapman uses the image of Odysseus's voyage again in Montsurry's great speech V.i, 60. *Cf.* Spenser's use of the same symbolism in *The Faerie Queene*, II.xii, Guyon's journey to the Bower of Blisse.

45 III.ii, 292. *monster-formed clouds*. Monsieur is only thinking of the hypocrisy with which women veil their illegal passions from the light of day, but his speech forms an ironic echo to Tamyra's lament at III.i, 59, 'Our bodies are but thick clouds to our souls.'

45 III.ii, 296. At this point B adds a new scene of sixty lines in which Monsieur discloses his fears of Bussy, and Maffé is developed as a comic character. The sequence is well written and carefully dove-tailed into the original. It could be by Chapman, but I think it would be against his sense of the decorum proper to tragedy to include such a scene. I have therefore followed A.

45 III.ii, 299. *Sybilla's cave*. Probably the Cumaean Sibyl whom Aeneas consulted before descending to the lower world; but the name was applied to a number of women with powers of prophecy.

45 III.ii, 301, *advanced valour*. Advanced against Monsieur and also given advancement by him.

45 III.ii, 302. *a spirit raised without a circle*. Without the circle which the magician normally drew around himself to protect him from the spirits he was conjuring. Chapman uses the same image in *The Teares of Peace* (674–5).

46 III.ii, 305. *what leapest thou at?* Presumably on seeing Monsieur, Bussy goes through the motions of reaching for a crown—'O royal object'—out of 'th' empty air'.

46 III.ii, 307. *Titan*. The sun god. Ferguson suggests that Bussy is comparing Monsieur's desire for the throne with Phaeton's wish to drive his father's chariot (p. 12). Phaeton was a generally accepted emblem of the fall of pride.

46 III.ii, 327. *if they be not made fools*. 'Do not think themselves wise, unless they hear their praises sung by others who, in reality, are making fools of them.' (Parrott.)

47 III.ii, 348. Ajax went mad with rage when Achilles' arms

were given to Ulysses and slaughtered a flock of sheep, thinking it to be the Grecian army.

47 III.ii, 353. *But stop at humours.* The rational soul is not strong enough to control all the functions and establish harmony among them, so that the four humours are free to do what they will, resulting in fluctuating and contradictory passions.

47 III.ii, 360. *carry.* Perhaps used in the sense of 'attribute'; 'your valour to which I attribute all your crimes.' But Monsieur may also be implying that he feeds Bussy's valour with all the discontent of Bussy's life so that it may break out into the biggest crime of all, the killing of the king.

47 III.ii, 364. *Jupiter Hammon.* Jacquot suggests that this is an allusion to the visit of Alexander the Great to the oracle of Jupiter Ammon. In his pride he wanted to be worshipped as the son of Jupiter.

47 III.ii, 365. *gall.* Not just a metaphor. The gall-bladder was thought to control the amount of choler in the blood: Bussy's discontent—(eat'st thy heart in vinegar)—adding to the natural bitterness of his gall, poisons his blood, and unbalances his humours by suppressing the choler and allowing the phlegm and melancholy to become excessive. This mars his complexion and produces a melancholy which breeds treachery and calumny, all of them being opposed to the pride produced by choler.

47 III.ii, 367. *toad-pool.* A stagnant pond in which toads engender, suggesting corruption and unhealthiness. *Cf. The Changeling.* II.i, 58.
complexion. Implying the older meaning, commixture of humours, as well as the modern sense of the word.

48 III.ii, 401. *Cf. The Revenge of Bussy:* 'Learn to kiss horror, and with death engender.' (I.ii, 32.)

48 III.ii, 406-7. *Clotho . . . Lachesis.* Two of the three Fates who span the thread of life. Clotho held the distaff. Lachesis drew out the thread and Atropos cut it off. Bussy imagines Clotho dropping her distaff in the dirt— *(rock:* distaff: *breathing:* giving life)—and Lachesis drawing off the dirty thread of Monsieur's life, making it still fouler as she does so by dipping her fingers in a bowl brimming (crowned) with human vices.

49 IV.i, 9-20. 'As the moon both reflects and influences the changeableness of women, so women, the most perfect images of the moon, set the pattern for and govern the

changes in the moods of men.' The passage is built up
through a series of parallels—'the moon, of all things God
created . . . women, that of all things made of nothing',
'the most appropriate image . . . the most perfect images'.
This is destroyed in B by the substitution of 'height' for
'light' (line 12) and 'idols' for 'images' (line 16). Chapman is drawing here on traditional Platonic sun-moon
symbolism, as defined by Leone Ebreo, for example, in
his *Philosophy of Love*, Dial. III, pp. 214–226 (ed. and
trans F. Friedeberg-Seeley and J. H. Barnes. London
1937.) The sun is male, pouring down his light upon the
receptive female moon: he is also the mind, while the
moon is the soul, intermediate between mind and body
and only truly herself when turned upwards towards the
light of reason. Bussy's flippant suggestion that women
rule in men, the moon governs the sun, carries with it the
implication that the wavering passions of the body have
more power than the divine light of reason—an idea stated
in the next twenty lines and illustrated throughout the
play. *Cf*. III.i, 59–67.

49   IV.i, 17. *moon-calves*. Children of the moon, but also carrying less complimentary meanings—idiots, abortions.

50   IV.i, 35. *these base foes*. This speech contains ironic echoes
of Bussy's contemptuous dismissal of sin at III.i, 18–21.
'Sin is a coward, Madam, and insults/But on our weakness', as well as of Tamyra's own sheltering behind the
shield of Nature (III.i, 47–50). Bussy is here admitting
while at the same time deploring the impotence of reason
against the 'natural' promptings of the blood.

50   IV.i, 37. *tyrannous law, treachery or beastly need*. These
presumably are the 'base foes' which, like grief, spring
from 'a natural sickness of the blood' i.e. an unbalance of
the humours. Having Nature behind them they are uncontrollable, though by themselves they would be nothing. The whole description is reminiscent of Monsieur's
analysis of Bussy in whom the unbalance of humours has
bred passions to which Bussy's valour is merely a slave.
(III.ii, 365–73.)

50   IV.i, 48–51. The sudden burst of rhyming couplets from
Tamyra in the middle of a scene of blank verse draws
attention to the fact that she is putting on an act.

50   IV.i, 52–6. Monsieur is taunting Bussy under cover of the
general exchanges of courtship. His references to Bussy's
valour (52) is an allusion to his character sketch of Bussy
in the previous scene, and his sneer at Bussy's 'great

eagle's beak' (54) refers back to Bussy's brag that he will thump the liver of wicked men (III.ii, 37). The liver here, however, is the seat of love.

50 IV.i, 59. *all men else.* Monsieur deliberately misconstrues Henry's speech, taking it to mean all men other than Bussy, instead of all men as well as Bussy. (Parrott.)

51 IV.i, 71. *armed his forehead.* Given horns to *Cf.* IV.i, 118. 'Married men's ensigns are not made with fingers.'

51 IV.i, 76. *Stretched in the arms.* Simultaneous reference to military and to sexual powers.

51 IV.i, 81. *Fed with bare coxcombs.* With doffing of caps and servile bowings. 'enchanted flames': cocks were frequently sacrificed in the rituals of witchcraft. *Cf.* the Lady Kyteler who brought the 'red combs of her cocks' to 'that insolent fiend, Robert Artessin'. (W. B. Yeats: *Nineteen hundred and nineteen.*)

51 IV.i, 85. *box-tree.* Noted both for its lowness and for its toughness. *Cf. Byron's Tragedy,* V.iii, 14. (Parrott.)

51 IV.i, 92. *Th'Armenian dragons.* The gold-guarding griffins of Scythia mentioned by Heroditus. (Parrott.)

51 IV.i, 96. *no proportioned end.* An especially ambiguous remark coming from Monsieur, in view of his argument with Guise at V.iii, 1, and in view, also, of the fact that he makes sure that Bussy does not outlive him. Proportioned: proportionate.

52 IV.i, 120. *a mere Cynthia.* A pure Cynthia, i.e. Diana, Goddess of Chastity and of the moon. Monsieur enjoys the paradox that the chaste moon should yet have horns, and that this Cynthia should be a giver of them.

52 IV.i, 125–7. Parrott suggests that Monsieur's paper is a love letter from Bussy stolen by Pero. Brooke, however, argues that Monsieur has written down what he swore to Pero he would not tell. (III.ii, 189.) Hence, 'I must not speak' (line 123) and IV.ii, 86—'what the wicked man hath written'.

53 IV.i, 144. *set looks.* 'Set' is a printing term, to set up in type.

53–4 IV.i, 149–58. This passage is heavily indebted to contemporary medical theory. The spirits (vegetable, vital and animal) were the link between body and soul and the means by which the three-fold soul controlled the bodily functions. They were concocted in the liver out of the purest blood, and could be transferred materially from one person to another through the physical senses in a stream of particles. In this way they were the means by

which 'soul into the soul may flow/Though it to bodies
first repair.' (See J. B. Bamborough, *The Little World
of Man*, Chap. III.) Here Tamyra has fainted because her
soul has been driven by her fear from its proper functions,
and Montsurry proposes to revive her by an infusion of
his own soul through a kiss. By line 157, however, he is
afraid that his 'troubled blood', resulting from the
inability of his own soul to establish harmony within his
own being, will infect her with a like chaos. She was all
harmony 'being best informed'—i.e. when his soul
reigned truly in her as in himself; but now before he can
help her he must first 'digest' his own confusions. 'Digest'
probably refers to the function of the liver in concocting
the spirits and humours in their proper harmonious
proportion.

54   IV.i, 174. 'If the slander comes from him, it is a thing of
beauty in me and proof of my innocence, as in the cases
of Bellerophon, Peleus and Hippolytus, who were all
falsely accused by lustful women as I by a lustful man.'

54   IV.i, 175. *Chimæra*. A monster slain by Bellerophon who,
having rejected the love of the wife of King Proteus, was
falsely accused by her and sent to kill the monster in the
expectation that he himself would be killed.
Peleus. A similar case; he rejected the love of Astydameia
who falsely accused him to her husband, Acastus. Acastus
took him hunting wild beasts on Mount Pelion and left
him defenceless without his sword, but he was saved by
Chiron, the Centaur.

54   IV.i, 177. *the chaste Athenian prince*. Hippolytus, accused
for the same reason by his step-mother, Phædra, and
therefore destroyed by Neptune's monsters at the prayer
of his father Theseus. He was raised from the underworld
by Aesculapius on the discovery of his innocence. Schoell
(pp. 41–42) points out that these three stories are grouped
together as examples of innocence in Comes, *Mytholo-
giae, De Bellerophonte*.

54   IV.i, 181–3. *Sacred Innocence*. 'Frightens those of whom
she is afraid, and puts to flight those who hunt her.'
Tamyra is referring to Monsieur's departure as soon as
she arrived: 'How his guilt shunned me.'

54   IV.i, 184–6. Both Jason and Cadmus sowed dragon's teeth
from which sprang a host of armed men. B makes the
reference clearer by emending line 185 to '. . . his ven-
omed teeth, from whose cursed seed', but omits the
characteristic pun on 'soil.'

55   IV.i, 197. *be not nice.* 'Don't have scruples and hesitate to pawn your honour for something you think is only a trifle, if it should have your honour vested in it.'

55   IV.i, 201. *Cerberus.* The three headed watch-dog guarding the gate of Hades. Hercules brought him up to the daylight as one of his labours. Tamyra is professing to be free from blemish by night or by day.

55   IV.i, 210. *powder.* In this context—'clear thy breast of me' —probably medicinal powder, a purge.

55   IV.i, 216. *To break his stock.* Brooke suggests 'stock' in the sense of property, hence, to bankrupt oneself, which agrees with playing 'a prodigal's part.'

55   IV.i, 217. *To cut a Gordian.* The knot which Alexander the Great cut with his sword when he could not untie it.

55   IV.i, 218–19. *to put true fire/to a false train.* Put a good light to a treacherous train of gunpowder, i.e. let your own true love to Tamyra drive you into dishonourable actions towards her.

55   IV.i, 222. *I'll attend your lordship.* Presumably Montsurry sets off with the intention of seeing Monsieur's paper, and Pero offers to go with him. B clarifies the situation by making Pero offer to go to Monsieur herself—'But I will to him'—an offer countermanded by Tamyra's decision to write him a letter.

56   IV.ii. B bridges the gap of time while Tamyra writes her letter by the introduction of eighteen lines of dialogue between Bussy and the friar, in which Bussy asks the friar to use his powers of magic. The Music of A, however, is still left in, probably by a mistake in the text.

56   IV.ii, 6. *all things to be feared, affrighted.* Boas and Parrott suggest 'By which all things capable of terror are frightened.' Brooke interprets more plausibly, 'Even creatures which one normally fears.'

56   IV.ii, 11. *Epimethean.* Epimetheus, the foolish brother of Prometheus who opened Pandora's box and let loose its evils upon mankind.

56   IV.ii, 16. *to wreak the sky.* To avenge Uranus—in Greek mythology the personification of the heavens and the father of the Titans. He was deposed by his son Chronos, who was in turn overthrown by his son Zeus, together with the rest of the Titans. In this war the Cyclops, the one-eyed giants, made thunderbolts for Zeus.

56   IV.ii, 27. *a raised spirit.* Not only raised by the friar's arts but also suggesting unfallen, angelic. There was much

controversy in the period about the legitimacy of using evil spirits as well as good in magic. The Hermetics believed that the truly virtuous magician could invoke all spirits with impunity, but all schools of magic agreed that it was dangerous to invoke the aid of spirits in unvirtuous causes. The friar's motives are of doubtful virtue and the spirit he invokes, Behemoth, was an extremely evil one. Behemoth was the infernal equivalent of Apollo, the sun. The fullest treatment of the subject is in Jacquot, *Bussy D'Amboise*, Introduction sec. VI.

57   IV.ii, 32–9. Parrott translates:
'Emperor of the legions of the spirits of the West, mighty Behemoth, appear, appear, attended by Ashtaroth, thy unvanquished lieutenant! I adjure thee by the inscrutable secrets of the Styx, by the irretraceable windings of Hell, be present, O Behemoth, thou for whom the cabinets of the mighty lie open. By the secret depths of Night and Darkness, by the wandering stars, by the stealthy march of the hours and Hecate's deep silence, come! Appear in spiritual form, gleaming, resplendent, lovely.'

57   IV.ii, 64. Stage direction. *A torch removes*. A clue to the method of staging 'these blue fires'.

58   IV.ii, 73. *great in our command*. 'Powerful in exercising command over us'. (Boas.) Parrott refers the phrase to 'spirit' hence, 'great in our host'.

58   IV.ii, 79. *No, be still and see*. Both A and B give this speech to Monsieur, but it must be spoken by Behemoth or the friar. It is typical of the equivocation of the fiend, that he never tells quite enough. They can *see* Monsieur, the Guise and Montsurry, but not hear what is being said.

58   IV.ii, 84. *fancy*. The faculty which sorted out sense perceptions and referred them to the reason for judgement or to the heart, for action.

58   IV.ii, 89. *a glass of ink*. 'A letter which, like a mirror, reflects Tamyra's unfaithfulness.' (Parrott.)

58   IV.ii, 91. *through all her paintings*. Monsieur pictures Tamyra as a painted woman whose flawed complexion can be seen through her paint. The image is perhaps suggested by that of Tragedy in the previous line making up for her part in front of the mirror.

58   IV.ii, 92. *gasping*. Brooke translates 'gaping', but there must also be a suggestion of the death bed in the image—at the last gasp.
fame's sepulchres. Her wrinkles which are the tomb of her good name.

59 IV.ii, 112. s.d. *Enter Pero with a letter.* The one which Tamyra gave her to deliver at IV.ii, 1.

60 IV.ii, 130. *stain.* A has 'stay' which B intelligently emended to 'dye'. Parrott suggested that 'stay' was a misprint for 'stayne'.

60 IV.ii, 144–6. *Lest fury . . . Accuse me.* 'Lest your anger too quickly aroused and the fact of your springing to my defence draws attention to our guilt.'

60 IV.ii, 154. *strow.* Cover up as they strewed rushes to cover the bare floor.

61 IV.ii, 160. *flanked.* Developed out of the metaphor of 'close mines' (line 155) which were tunnels dug underground beneath an enemy's position and containing a charge of gunpowder. Bussy sees the plots of Monsieur and himself as two such mines dug parallel to each other from opposite directions.

61 IV.ii, 161. *the feeling centre.* The earth, the centre of the Ptolemaic universe. (*Cf.* the still 'Centre' II.ii, 165, 'the green centre,' IV.ii, 170.) 'Feeling': sensitive, conscious.

61 IV.ii, 163. *inspired.* 'Blown on', linked with 'weather'—i.e. bad weather, storms; but also implying inspiration, possessing prophetic powers. The thresholds will sweat in anticipation of his coming as stones drip with condensation and foretell the coming storm.

61 IV.ii, 169. *the superficies.* The outside of the green earth. The green fields on the surface are contrasted with the ploughing up of hell by the politician which goes on below and from which the harvest of policy springs. The image of mining underground (line 155) is still present.

61 V.i. B. adds four lines of dialogue at the start of the scene giving a more effective dramatic opening.

61 V.i, 13. *The stony birth of clouds.* Thunderbolts, as also 'the wild seed of vapour' (line 16). It was a common belief that lightning never struck a laurel tree or a sleeping person.

62 V.i, 38–40. There is a complex mixture of Christian and classical allusion in these and the following lines. Because of his suffering and because he is about to take a course which the friar has denounced as un-Christian, Montsurry cries out like 'a soul in hell', lacking the faith which can remove mountains or open the seven-times-heated furnace. (Daniel III, 19.) He may also be equating himself with the fallen giants whom Jove crushed under mountains. (*Cf.* note on V.iii, 182–188.)

62   V.i, 40. *set fit outcries*. The O.E.D. gives for 'set', 'to write a musical composition for certain voices'. The music is the outcries, the voice that of the damned soul.

62   V.i, 41. *it nothing fits*. 'Speaking isn't enough; it needs thunder or the last trump to express my cares.'

62   V.i, 43–9. *The trump of Heaven*. Montsurry feels that his outcry should anticipate ('prevent' with a further play on 'vented', 46) the last trumpet which heralds the end of the world, kills the living and calls up the dead. Again there is the further reference to the fallen giants crushed under the mountains who, according to classic myth, were the cause of volcanoes; hence 'hot woes . . . vented . . . vapour' (lines 45–6).

63   V.i, 55. *Hereafter*. Montsurry converts Tamyra's 'here-after' into a vision of an endless future in which the thought of her infidelity will perpetually continue to arise in his mind.

63   V.i, 57. *Fame grows in going*. Taken from the Aeneid, IV, 173–5. The scandal will get greater as it goes along.

63   V.i, 57–9. *scapes*. Escapades, sins. 'The excuses which virtue makes for her slips only serve to damn her all the more, though they would be accepted in the case of an ordinary person.'

63   V.i, 60. *Come, Siren*. Montsurry proposes to use Tamyra as the Siren to lure 'thy ruffian galley'—Bussy—to destruction against the rocks—himself.

63   V.i, 61. *rigged with quench for lust*. A has 'laden for thy lust'. I have retained the version in B because of its verbal parallel to *The Revenge of Bussy* (I.ii, 27–9): 'This blood . . ./Too dry is to breed any quench to thine./ And therefore now (if only for thy lust) . . .' Also the pun on 'rigged' is typical of Chapman: 'rigged' of a ship, and 'rig', to play the wanton. *Cf. Antony and Cleopatra*, 'Bless her when she is riggish.' (II.ii, 248.)

63   V.i, 62–5. Montsurry's sexual obsession in this speech comes out through the traditional 'fish-mongering' imagery of 'nets', 'spawn', reinforced by reference to 'lap', i.e.: genital organs. (*Cf.* IV.i, 180, and *Hamlet*, III.ii, 120.) 'To dance in a net' was a popular proverb meaning to delude oneself that one's actions were secret when in fact they were not (Tilley. N. 130, p. 496); but behind the whole sequence also is a reference to Mars and Venus caught in Vulcan's net.

63   V.i, 66. *quit . . . sleight*. To repay his virility by a woman's

trick, i.e. summoning Bussy to his death by Tamyra's letter.

63　V.i, 67. *Who never is deceived in her deceit.* 'Who' presumably refers to Bussy who is going to be deceived by this particular trick though he is not normally 'deceived in her deceit'—i.e.: not taken in by the show of chastity and virtue which she puts on but which she doesn't intend him to take seriously.

63　V.i, 70. *That ever lapped.* A pun on 'lap' (line 63) as well as a reference to the dog returning to its vomit. Montsurry plans to see the pander when he next returns to the scene of his crime.

63　V.i, 71–2. *That I may see the devil . . . wive.* This sounds like a proverbial saying, perhaps containing some reference to the devil and his dam. It may be an allusion to *Dr. Faustus* (II.i, 141) where Faustus, having sold his soul to the devil, at once asks for a wife and is given a woman-devil: 'Here's a hot whore indeed.'

63　V.i, 73–4. *That I may hang him.* The reference is to hanging, drawing and quartering of criminals.

63　V.i, 77. *for all the comets.* Comets were omens of disaster. Men cannot escape from the beauty of a woman's face in spite of the warning given by all the great disasters stemming from it. See also Introduction p. xxvii for the symbolism of comets in the play.

63　V.i, 80. *basilisks.* A fabulous reptile whose breath and look were said to be poisonous.

63　V.i, 81. *coast.* Picked up from the original ship image— 'ruffian galley'.'No way of making an easy voyage to their hearts.'

63　V.i, 84. *in human state.* Brooke comments on the relevance of this to one of the play's central themes, 'the necessity of "animal" passion to "human" nature.' The whole sequence defines the human state in a series of paradoxes —'stayed . . . fettered', 'secure . . . cares', 'human . . . beasts', which express in concentrated form Chapman's sense of the conflict and complexity of life.

63　V.i, 86. *Pelion and Cythaeron.* Mountains in Greece noted for their wild beasts. An echo of *Hercules Oetaeus* (line 269) where Dejanira in her jealousy describes the wild beasts she carries in her breast.

64　V.i, 96–7. *this ruthless steel—this impartial torture.* The knife and the rack, without pity, without favour to anyone.

64　V.i, 99. *To quicken life in dying.* How to keep life going when torture has almost destroyed it.

64 V.i, 121–2. *Where all these.* i.e. manhood, noblesse and religion. They may be restored by carrying out their just revenge in the place where they were lost.

65 V.i, 126. *Thy right of sufferance.* 'The right by which you are made to suffer.' Jacquot points out that 'sufferance' is a legal term meaning the condition of holding on to an estate after one's legal right to it has expired, and also, the legitimate penalty to which one is exposed by such a crime. Tamyra, though claiming the rights of a wife, has lost her 'privilege in lust' and is paying the legal penalty: hence Montsurry's insistence on the legality of his revenge and his 'impartial' torture. He puns savagely on the word 'right', presumably stabbing with each use of the word.

65 V.i, 130. *Dissolve yourself again.* Blood was supposed to have special properties as a solvent. Browne refutes the vulgar error that the blood of a goat could dissolve the hardest stone. (*Pseudodoxia,* II.v.) There is also a tradition of religious symbolism behind the image—the blood of Christ dissolving the stony tablets of the law. *Cf.* Herbert: 'If stony hearts will melt with gentle love' (*The Sacrifice*). Tamyra's plea for mercy would seem to be invoking this.

65 V.i, 132–4. 'The more monstrously I behave, the more I resemble you; thus in stabbing you again I am expressing and portraying your monstrosity in my own.'

65 V.i, 135. *thy monstrous idol is not done yet.* From her initial reference to the Gorgon, Tamyra suggested that Montsurry was growing into a stone statue representing Tyranny—'the image of all tyranny' (131). Montsurry takes up the metaphor: the statue is not finished yet by the use of the dagger, 'this tool'; he will complete the image and transform himself completely by the use of the rack.

65 V.i, 140–2. *Thy venoms soaked through.* Ferguson (p. 13) suggests that Chapman is thinking of the poisoned shirt of Nessus by which Dejanira unwittingly killed Hercules, and of her subsequent desire to be hurled from a steep cliff in expiation of her crime. (*Hercules Oetaeus,* 863.)

65 V.i, 146. A fine dramatic touch when Tamyra in the agony of the wrack turns instinctively to her husband for help.

65 V.i, 148. *Oh, wrack of nature.* The friar dies on a pun—rack and wrack. 'Wrack' has a variety of meanings, including wreck, punishment, revenge, all of which are relevant. The friar dies of shock and horror—'for thought' (line

170); hence Behometh's riddling statement that he was not slain but died a natural death (V.ii, 59).

66　V.i, 153. *earth moves.* A reference to Copernicus. *Cf. Teares of Peace,* 215–16. The subsequent image is of a bowl whose bias has caused it to rotate. In the same way the weight of religious hypocrisy—'the gravity of her religious face'—has caused the earth to turn over and reveal the sins and diseases behind. Possibly the image is pointed by the fact of the holy friar lying face downwards with the open vault beside him. 'Earth moves and heaven stands still.'

66　V.i, 173. *his.* Man's. *Cf.* lines 84–5, the human state which includes the necessity of animal passions.

67　V.ii In B, A's V.iii, 1–56 is inserted as V.ii; A's V.ii becomes V.iii, and A's V.iii, 57 to end, becomes V.iv.

67　V.ii, 5–7. The ceiling seems to rise higher and the floor to fall away beneath him. (Brooke.)

67　V.ii, 15. *his utmost weed.* His outer garment which Montsurry has taken as a disguise.

67　V.ii, 26. *spirit.* Used in a double sense; referring to Behemoth who has promised aid, and to the animal spirits which rose from the heart to the brain and made it active.

67　V.ii, 28. *his free and gentle vow.* There is great irony in Bussy's applicatien of these terms to Behemoth, an evil spirit, ruler of the western legions—i.e. the spirits of the setting sun (IV.ii, 32) who, when first called to appear, hated the 'accursed light' (IV.ii, 46). His warnings, as in IV.ii, are either too cryptic to be understood or else clearer but certain to be ignored.

68　V.ii, 39. *Terror of darkness.* Bussy invokes first the sun-god, the bringer of light, to dispel the darkness which enshrouds the oracle, and then, in case of failure, the Prince of darkness who can see in darkness and hence may reveal the nature of the oracle from within. Dilke, puzzled why Bussy should invoke the light at all when he said he was going to summon Behemoth, emends 'Or' (line 45) to 'Oh', making the whole invocation to the Prince of darkness alone, and the flames in line 39 to be the flames of hell. Lines 40–3, however, can only apply to a spirit of light and we must assume that Bussy invokes both. His double invocation accords very closely with the common Renaissance distinction between Natural and Demoniac magic as defined, for example, in Pico della Mirandola's

Oration on the Dignity of Man, Sec. 32–3, pp. 246–49. (*The Renaissance Philosophy of Man*, ed. Kristeller, Chicago, 1948.) The former is noble, wedding earth to heaven by exploiting the 'reciprocal affinity of natures' which exists between the higher and lower levels of the universe. The latter makes use of evil spirits and so makes the magician their slave. Bussy appears not to recognize the difference between the two, and Chapman, making the evil spirit answer his call but not the good, gives a warning of the tragic outcome.

68   V.ii, 40. *thy music-footed horse*. The horses drawing the chariot of Apollo who was also the god of music. The crystal would refer to the crystalline sphere of the Ptolemaic system with which the sun revolved. Jacquot suggests a reference to Pegasus who caused to spring up by a blow of his hoof the fountain Hippocrene, sacred to the Muses.

68   V.ii, 42. *instructive fire*. Pico calls Natural magic 'the utter perfection of natural philosophy' by which the magician 'brings forth into the open the miracles concealed in the recesses of the world, in the depths of nature, and in the storehouses and mysteries of God.' (*Op. Cit.* Sec. 33, p. 249.)

69   V.ii, 62. *A fit pair of shears*. A reference to Atropos. *Cf.* note on III.ii, 406–7.

69   V.ii, 64. *consorts*. Partners: also instruments or musicians playing together.

69   V.ii, 69. *My death consenting*. 'Even if my death fulfils his prophecy.'

69   V.ii, 76. *even to many deaths*. Carrying the common sexual double meaning of the period.

69   V.ii, 84. *O lying spirit*. Behemoth, because Bussy thinks he has lied about the friar's death.

69   V.ii, 91. *elixir*. The alchemist's preparation designed to turn base metal to gold: hence able to change a prostitute into a virtuous woman and make chastity her essence, as heat is the essence of fire. Also a preparation for prolonging life eternally, and used in a general sense to mean 'quintessence'. All these senses are present. The 'spirits' were formed from the quintessence of the blood and enabled the body to perform its functions: Hence 'how it multiplies my blood with spirit.' *Cf.* IV.i, 149, note.

70   V.ii, 93. *all the signs*. possibly the signs of the zodiac, the constellations governing man's life.

70 V.ii, 97. The scene closes with strong dramatic irony as Bussy goes to his death.

70 V.iii. B moves the opening debate between Monsieur and Guise to the beginning of Sc. II, and replaces the choric role of the two characters by a dramatic one. For this reason, perhaps, the leisurely simile, lines 5–12, appropriate to a chorus, is cut down in B to the more dramatic brevity of three lines. For the relevance of the opening debate to the play as a whole see the Introduction, p. xix.

70 V.iii, 14. *the mere necessity of matter.* The conditions imposed by the very nature of the matter she is working in.

70–1 V.iii, 17–25. The debate is ostensibly about whether nature works at random, but Monsieur goes further than this, arguing that real nobility is a positive handicap in the world and likely to destroy its possessor, whereas mere worthlessness stands safe.

71 V.iii, 30. *decorum.* Chapman may be thinking of Horace's example of indecorum of a figure with a body of one kind and a head of another.

71 V.iii, 38. *full-manned.* Possessing all human virtues, the 'full creature' of line 46. Also a pun developing out of the image of ships of war (line 21).

71 V.iii, 49–56. These lines are closely adapted from Seneca's *Agememnon,* lines 64–72. *Lybian sands:* the north African coast famous for its sand-banks. *The Euxine Sea:* the Black Sea. *Bootes;* The Waggoner; a northern constellation near to the Great Bear, alternatively named the Wagon and Septemtriones, the seven ploughing oxen. Hence Bootes' 'radiant team.'

71 V.iii, 56. At this point in B, Montsurry enters with murderers and has a brief conversation with Monsieur about the plot in hand, before all exeunt to end the scene. In A, Monsieur and Guise remain above in silence awaiting the outcome. In B, they enter above at line 75 and are given short speeches to make them part of a realistic dramatic pattern.

71 V.iii, 57. *Revive these stupid thoughts.* 'Recover your thoughts from the stupor they are in.'

71 V.iii, 58–60. *Gathering . . . an idle fancy.* 'Brooding over the horrors but doing nothing about it.'

72 V.iii, 63. *Blow . . . engaged.* 'Sound the signal for his retreat before the fight begins.'

72 V.iii, 71–4. These lines are omitted in B, presumably

because they serve no direct dramatic purpose. Their stoicism, however, is so typical of Chapman at the time of writing *The Revenge of Bussy* that it is difficult to believe that he himself could have been the reviser who dropped them.

72   V.iii, 81–2. *Who dares give all the room . . . reach.* 'Who dares come even within sight of me when I have my weapon in hand, or face up to me in fight whatever the odds in his favour?'

72   V.iii, 84. B adds lines here which it is tempting to keep. 'If I scape Monsieur's 'pothecary shops,/Foutre for Guise's shambles.'—an echo of Bussy's reference to 'politic Monsieur or the violent Guise' of V.ii, 82. Whether or not Chapman wrote them, he only found it possible to include them in the B version when Monsieur and the Guise are still active agents in the plot and egg the murderers on. They would be out of place in the A arrangement in view of the depersonalized role which the two characters have by this time taken on.

73   V.iii, 92. *Will it not enter here?* Presumably the murderer is wearing armour so that Bussy has to stab him in the face.

73   V.iii, 99. *a speeding sleight and well resembled.* An effective trick and clever impersonation.

73   V.iii, 110. *where it would protect.* Brooke suggests that 'it' refers to 'her renown.' I would refer it to 'a life', Bussy's life which is above reproach and affords a sanctuary for whoever it seeks to protect.

73   V.iii, 112. *enforce the spot.* 'Emphasize the stain on your honour.' (Boas.)

74   V.iii, 129. *these divines.* The divine parts are only for show not use. Also a pun on divines, preachers, who claim the pre-eminence of the soul.

74   V.iii, 130–1. *two sweet courtly friends . . . A mistress and a servant.* Mind and blood, soul and body. 'courtly' leads into the cynicism of 'a courtier's breath' (line 132) which is all that life amounts to. There is irony in the use, at this moment, of the image of courtship, mistress and servant, all so closely associated with the love affair which has brought Bussy to his death. Who, in fact, is the mistress and who the servant in this relationship of mind and blood?

74   V.iii, 133–4. *Nothing . . . shade.* 'Everything is created out of nothing and returns to nothing again; hence the essence of life is just an illusion based on an empty shadow.' *Cf.* I.i, 18–19: ' a dream/But of a shadow.'

74 V.iii, 137–40. *And if Vespasian.* Added in B. The episode is mentioned in Grimestone's – *General Inventorie* (1607), p. 990 which Chapman was using for his *Revenge of Bussy* about the time of the revision of *Bussy D'Ambois.* The lines, therefore, are probably authentic.

74 V.iii, 142–3. *The equal thought.* Bussy brags that he looks with stoical impartiality on life and death alike; hence he stands upright supported by two equal props and inclining to neither side. *Cf. Hercules Oetaeus*, 1741–2. Hercules, rising in the midst of the flames, bending his tortured limbs to neither side.

74 V.iii, 143. *I am up.* I use Boas' punctuation. Both A and B read 'I am up/Here like a Roman statue; I will stand/ Till death . . . marble:'

74 V.iii, 147–53. Closely adapted from *Hercules Oetaeus*, 1518–26, where the Chorus beg the sun to broadcast the death of Hercules to the whole world:

> 'O glory of the world, O ray-girt Sun, at whose first warmth Hecate loosens the bits from the weary steeds of her nocturnal car, tell the Sabaeans who lie beneath the dawn, tell the Iberians who lie beneath thy setting, tell those who suffer neath the Wagon of the Bear, and those who pant beneath thy burning car: Hercules is hasting to the endless shades . . .' (Loeb.)

74 V.iii, 147–8. *the grey-eyed morn . . . Sabaean spices.* The east. Saba was the chief city of the Yemen whose merchants were famous for their traffic in spices and perfumes.

74 V.iii, 149. *Iberian vales.* The west. The Iberian peninsula.

74 V.iii, 150. *Hecate.* Goddess of the infernal regions, darkness, witchcraft. Linked with oak-trees perhaps through druidical rites.

74 V.iii, 152. *The burning axle-tree.* The axle-tree was the imaginary line round which the Ptolemaic system revolved. 'Burning': the equator, to which the sun comes nearest in its circuit.

74 V.iii, 153. *the snowy Bear. Cf. Hercules Oetaeus*, line 1584: 'glacialis ursae'. The Pole star is in the constellation, the Little Bear, but both the Great and the Little Bear were associated with the figure of the wagon—'the chariot'.

74–5 V.iii, 155–8. The image is of the volley fired over a hero's grave. 'Worthless' has the double sense of 'futile, without meaning', and 'not according to my worth.'

75 V.iii, 161. Bussy's gift of his sword echoes Hercules' gift of his bow and arrows to Philoctetes. *Hercules Oetaeus*, 1648.

75 V.iii, 165. *spirit.* Both the animal spirits, the source of

Bussy's valour, and the spirits—i.e. essences—refined by the alchemists. 'Stilled' can mean both 'distilled from' and 'instilled into.'

75   V.iii, 167. *spleen.* The spleen was associated both with melancholy and mirth. Here, since 'impartial', it presumably means temper, habit of mind. 'May the weight of my blood in one scale outweigh the penalty in the other which my noble love has incurred.'

75   V.iii, 182–7. *My sun is turned to blood.* There are analyses of this difficult speech of the dying Bussy in Ferguson, pp. 15–17, and in Jacquot, *Bussy D'Amboise,* Intro. xcviii-ix and pp. 199–200. Chapman seems to have had in mind a number of passages from *Hercules Oetaeus* as well as some verses from *Revelation.* Two passages from Seneca in particular which Jacquot believes to have been telescoped in Chapman's mind by the word 'ossa' in both, as well as by their common reference to Hercules' death are (1) Hercules' description of the pains he suffers in the fire which has destroyed his very bones: 'Nec ossa durant ipsa'. (line 1228) and (2) Hercules' plea to Jove to release the Titans and let them crush him under Pindus and Ossa as they themselves had been crushed, so that he may be freed from his pain (1307–10): 'Or, if thy hand shrinks reluctant from the impious task, 'gainst me release from Aetna's mount the burning Titans, who in their hands may heave Pindus up, or Ossa, thee, and by the hurled mountain overwhelm me quite.' (Loeb.) There would also seem to be references to *Revelation,* Chap. VI, 12 'and the moon became as blood'—hence 'this prodigy' (line 181), and also to Chap. VIII, verses 8, 10 and 11, describing the destruction of the world: 'a great mountain burning with fire was cast into the sea: and the third part of the sea became blood; . . . and there fell a great star from heaven . . . and many men died of the waters, because they were made bitter.' The combination of Christian and Senecan is the same as in Montsurry's speech, V.i, 38–49. Bussy's 'sun turned to blood' is Tamyra, as she shows him her wounds, the sight of which kills him as the murderers never could. As he looks at her bleeding breasts, therefore, he feels like the dying Hercules looking out over Pindus and Ossa, neighbouring peaks to Oeta upon which his funeral pyre was built. The thought of his failure, however, makes him feel unworthy of the role of Hercules, and identify himself instead with the Titans crushed under Pindus and Ossa,

and the two peaks become identified with Tamyra's wounded breasts which lie like mountains on his heart and liver, the seat of passion and emotion. It is a moment of great bitterness for Bussy that he, once the wielder of Jove's thunderbolt, should have suffered the fate which Monsieur predicted for him, to be struck 'under th'Etna of his pride'. (III.ii, 139.) The melting veins and the 'endless snow' suggest both the flowing of Tamyra's blood and his own ebbing vigour. Ferguson points out, however, that classic myth explained volcanoes by the fact of fallen giants under them, and the hungry torrents eating rocks may contain a reference to the lava produced by the heat of Bussy's passion which is great enough to melt mountains and poison the whole world. At the same time, the echoes of the bitter waters of *Revelation* recall the day of judgment and the burning out of Bussy's earthly part before the final regeneration which the friar prophesies for him at the end of the play. Bussy himself, however, has no idea of this and sees himself, in his death, as an emblem of human weakness for all mankind (lines 188–91).

75   V.iii, 191. *like a falling star.* For the nature of falling stars see Aristotle. *Meteorologica* I,iv. For the significance of the image at this point of the play see Introduction (p. xxviii) and Ferguson, p. 18.

76   V.iii, 194. *my unrested soul.* The friar has come from Purgatory having learned of his errors and having, as his initial penance, to undo some of the evil he has helped to create (lines 265–7). His task is to bring about a general forgiveness, to induce Bussy to forgive his murderers and effect a 'Christian reconcilement' between Tamyra and Montsurry (lines 199–201). When this is completed he goes back to undergo his own purgation (line 265). Significantly lines 265–7 are omitted from the speech in B. *Son of the earth.* The base earthly quality and the 'blind rage of blood' as opposed to 'the faith of heaven' and the higher nature of the fixed stars.

76   V.iii, 210. *O wretched piety.* Brooke points out that Chapman is here adapting a speech of Hyllus to Dejanira. *Hercules Oetaeus*, lines 1027–30.

76   V.iii, 223–5. *honoured.* The first means 'honourable', the second, 'respected.' Tamyra is repeating a central theme of the play, that real virtue and worldly success do not coincide.

77   V.iii, 252–61. *And as this taper.* In this very formal parting,

Montsurry makes of the candle a three-fold emblem signifying the death of their love. As its flame burns upwards yet consumes downwards, so Montsurry with his heart full of forgiveness and his hands held up to heaven yet feels bound to repudiate his love. As the candle burns and gives light, so it also destroys itself: as its flame burns clearly when pointing to heaven, so it is smothered when turned in the wrong direction. These are all traditional applications of a traditional symbol: *Cf. Othello* V.ii, 7.

77   V.iii, 254. *As, having lost his honey.* This refers to the wax of the candle which still retains some savour of the honey and a spice of its first parents, the bees, until it is extinguished.

77   V.iii, 257. *It sees and dies.* Brooke draws attention to the deeper implications of this passage. The candle is the emblem of the Fall, like life, looking upwards and consuming downwards, and the reference to 'his first parents' inevitably suggests Adam and Eve. It symbolizes that falling away from the first sweetness through original sin, but its final flare represents the 'final clarity of vision in the moment of death'—hence '*sees* and dies.' While accepting the general symbolism of the Fall in the passage, I cannot accept this interpretation of 'sees.' Bussy himself dies in despair not in a moment of such vision, and Montsurry, the speaker, is incapable of experiencing it. 'Sees' must surely be a reference to Genesis III, verses 5 and 7, where Adam and Eve ate of the apple and their eyes were opened and they knew death: '. . . in the day ye eat thereof, then your eyes shall be opened . . . And the eyes of them both were opened.' The winking eye of the candle symbolizes not the final vision of truth but the whole sorry declension of man from the prelapsarian state.

77   V.iii, 261–2. Brooke retains the punctuation of A: 'so let our love,/Now turne from me, as here I turn from thee.' I prefer Boas' emendation which keeps the pattern of strong stops after each 'So let our love', and emphasizes the three distinct emblematic uses of the candle.

78   V.iii, 268–74. *Farewell.* In B, this speech is moved back to line 194, immediately after the death of Bussy. The A version is immeasurably more effective, concentrating the attention on the great central figure of the play and prophesying a final regeneration which follows logically from the preceding scenes of forgiveness.

78   V.iii, 268. *brave relicts of a complete man*. Possibly Chapman
       has in mind the constant references in *Hercules Oetaeus*
       to the diminution of Hercules' giant size through the
       poison of the shirt of Nessus and the flames of the pyre.
       e.g.: lines 1343–5. relicts: remains.

78   V.iii, 269–70. *Look up*. See *Hercules Oetaeus*, lines 1564–71,
       the chorus' prophecy that Hercules will be made a star,
       and lines 1940–43, Hercules' confirmation from above
       that he has become one.

78   V.iii, 271. *the firmament*. A term used loosely to include all
       the celestial spheres of the Ptolemaic system as well as the
       specific eighth sphere which was that of the fixed stars.
       The friar exhorts the spirit of Bussy to burst through the
       enclosing sub-lunar sphere and setting the whole system
       aflame, begin a new cosmic cycle and bring back the
       Golden Age. For possible connections with Bruno, see
       Introduction (pp. xxiv).

78   V.iii, 272. *cracked*. A has 'cracke'. The emendation is
       Brooke's.

TEXTUAL APPENDIX

Comparison of 1607 quarto (A) with that of 1641, (B)

Act I, Scene i

5	A, incessant; B, continual.
8	A, forging; B, forming.
10	A, our tympanous statists; B, men merely great.
20	A, powers; B, wealth.
25	A, glad; B, fain.
31	A, world; B, earth.
40	A, poor; B, mean.
43	A, likely; B, possible.
44	A, fit I get; B, good to get.
57	A, Thinkest; B, Callest.
80	A, doth; B, do.
82	A, wish me do; B, wish me.
83	A, as; B, where.
92	A, portly; B, humorous.
110	A, eyes; B, loves.
113	A, rude; B, old.
117	A, ruled; B, wise.
122–6	Added in B.
126	A, But he's no husband here; a smooth plain ground.
130	A, with; B, for.
144	A, man; B, wretch.
152	A, I serve; B, I do serve.
156	A, A pass; B, His pass.
157	A, good fashion; B, respect.
165	A, a poet; B, some poet.
167	A, his wise Excellency; B, your great master's goodness.
170	A, bad; B, rude.
180	A, Highness'; B, Grace's.
187	A, scholar; B, poet.
192	A, his Excellence; B, his bounteous Grace.
193	A, to your deserts/The reverend virtues of a faithful steward; B, to you of long ones.
197	A, merry; B, pleasant.
198	A, believe it; B, by'rlady.
200	A, my Lord; B, his Grace.

208   B adds:

> *Bussy.* How, Ambo, sir?
> *Maffé.*   Ay, is not your name Ambo?
> *Bussy.* You call'd me lately D'Ambois; has your Worship
> So short a head?
> *Maffé.*   I cry thee mercy, D'Ambois.

210   A, Serve God, play the good husband; B, If you be thrifty
       and play the good husband.

220   A, sown; B, set.

       Act I, Scene ii
  2   A, this; B, that.
  4   A, under hand; B, under the hand.
 10   A, form; B, fashion.
 11   A, semi-gods; B, demigods.
 13   B adds:

> *Montsurry.* No question she's the rarest queen in Europe.
> *Guise.* But what's that to her immortality?

 16   A, boast; B, vaunt.
 18   A, rudeness; B, clowneries.
 30   A, deformity; B, confusion. A, sight; B, eyes.
 45   A, first born; B, sole heir.
51–3   B emends:

> But they have faults, and we more; they foolish proud
> To jet in others plumes so haughtily;
> We proud that they are proud of foolery,
> Holding our worths more complete for their vaunts.

 55   A, this gentleman t' attend you; B, a gentleman to Court.
 59   A, I; B, We.
 60   A, I; B, We.
 64   A, He; B, They. B omits 'She's not shameless'.
 68   A, my love; B, sweetheart.
 71   B adds: *Bussy.* 'Save you, Ladies'.
 78   B adds:

> *Henry.* Mark, Duchess of Guise, there is one is not bashful.
> *Duchess.* No, my lord, he is much guilty of the bold extremity.

 85   After 'princely colours', B adds:

> *Enter* BARRISOR, L'ANOU, *and* PYRHOT.
>
> *Duchess.* Soft, sir, you must rise by degrees, first being the
> servant of some common lady, or knight's wife, then a little
> higher to a lord's wife, next a little higher to a countess, yet a
> little higher to a duchess, and then turn the ladder.
> *Bussy.* Do you allow a man, then, four mistresses, when the
> greatest mistress is allowed but three servants?

> *Duchess.* Where find you that statute, sir?
> *Bussy.* Why, be judged by the groom-porters.
> *Duchess.* The groom-porters?
> *Bussy.* Ay, madam; must not they pledge of all gamings i' th' Court?
> *Duchess.* You talk like a gamester.

94   A, Madam; B, princely mistress.
95   B adds: 'Another riddle.'
98   A, Good; B, young.
101–6 B places these two speeches after 'cutting of mine', 112, and replaces 'more courtship, as you love it' by 'Another riddle', 106, omitting 113, 'So, sir, so.'

121   A, courtship; B, courting.
141   A, Ardor; B, Their heat.
142   A, and; B, but.
155   A, come new; B, newly drawn out.
162   A, roaring; B, braying.
167   A, for his honour; B, for his honour sake.
182   A, strange credulity; B, miraculous jealousy. B gives the speech to Barrisor.
184   A, into our merriment; B, into the matter of our merriment.
185   B spoken by L'Anou.
187   B spoken by Pyrhot.
188   A, with; B, in.
193   A, kill's outright; B, kill's outright else.
212   A, Come follow us; B, follow us.

Act II, Scene i

s.d. A, Henry, Guise, Beaumond, Nuntius; B, Henry, Guise, Montsurry and Attendants.
11   A, When; B, Where.
27   A, his; B, their.
120   A, quick an eye; B, swift a foot.
133   A, All slain outright?; B, all slain outright but he?
135   A, feebled; B, freckled.
136   A, cheeks; B, lips.
166   A, full; B, true.
185   A, violent; B, daring.
193   A, God; B, law.
204   A, no king; B, no law.
207   B omits 'Mort Dieu'.
210–11 B omits these two speeches and adds:

> *Monsieur.* [Now vanish horrors into Court attractions
> For which let this balm make thee fresh and fair.]
> And now forth with thy service to the Duchess,

As my long love will to Montsurry's Countess.   [*Exit.*
   Bussy. To whom my love hath long been vow'd in heart,
Although in hand for shew I held the Duchess.
And now through blood and vengeance, deeds of height,
And hard to be achiev'd, 'tis fit I make
Attempt of her perfection; I need fear
No check in his rivality, since her virtues
Are so renown'd, and he of all dames hated.   [*Exit.*

Act II, Scene ii
B omits lines 1–50 and begins the scene at 51, 'Pray thee regard.'

71 A, weighing a dissolute; B, joining a loose.
76 A, solemn; B, common.
111 A gives Tamyra's speech in this line to Montsurry.
135 A, profit; B, honour.
146 This line added in B.
147 A and B, wave.
158 A, all the; B, all ye.
173 B, For life's mere death, loving one that loathes me,
177–9 B emends:

See, see, a vault is opening that was never
Known to my lord and husband, nor to any
But him that brings the man I love, and me.
How shall I look on him? How shall I live,
And not consume in blushes? I will in,
And cast myself off, as I ne'er had been.

263 A, sits; B, wakes.
271 A, Was something troubled; B, Made some deep scruple.
272 A, hand; B, honour.
275–6 B expands to:

And therefore made his quarrel, his long love
And service, as I hear, being deeply vow'd
To your perfections; which my ready presence,
Presum'd on with my father at this season

281 A, comfort; B, good.

Act III, Scene i
B opens with new s.d. and two lines by Bussy before Tamyra speaks:

   Enter D'AMBOIS, TAMYRA, *with a Chain of Pearl.*
   Bussy. Sweet mistress, cease, your conscience is too nice,
And bites too hotly of the Puritan spice.

26 A, goddess; B, servile.
32 A, in our one; B, in one.
33 A, my truth; B, myself.

35 A, men; B, one.

In B, Bussy remains on stage at line 42, and 17 lines are
added before Tamyra begins her soliloquy:

Now let us call my father, whom I swear
I could extremely chide, but that I fear
To make him so suspicious of my love
Of which, sweet servant, do not let him know
For all the world.
   Bussy.   Alas, he will not think it!
   Tamyra. Come, then.—Ho! Father, ope, and take your friend.
                               [*Ascendit* FRIAR.
   Friar. Now, honour'd daughter, is your doubt resolv'd?
   Tamyra. Ay, father, but you went away too soon.
   Friar. Too soon?
   Tamyra.   Indeed you did, you should have stay'd;
Had not your worthy friend been of your bringing,
And that contains all laws to temper me,
Not all the fearful danger that besieg'd us,
Had aw'd my throat from exclamation.
   Friar. I know your serious disposition well.
Come, son, the morn comes on.
   Bussy.   Now, honour'd mistress,
Till farther service call, all bliss supply you!
   Tamyra. And you this chain of pearl, and my love only!
                   [*Descendit* FRIAR *and* D'AMBOIS.

73 A, thy beauties; B, thine eyes.
99 A, underneath the king; B, under our king's arm.

Act III, Scene ii

  1 A, my Bussy; B, Bussy.
  4 A, nothing; B, sparrows.
 16 A, truth; B, man.
 29 A, than; B, by.
 53 A, oppressed; B, besieged.
 58 A, t'other; B, rest.
 67 A, charge; B, bout.
 76 A, noblie; B, nobly.
 89 A, equal; B, honoured.
 96 A, eminence; B, empire.
104 A, plucked out one stick; B, plucked one stick out.
105 A, was comprisee; B, bound our lives.
107 A, ingenuous; B, ingenious.
117 A, prove the Hermean rod; B, hold the Hermean virtue.
121 A, Engender not; B, Decline not to.
130 B adds the following before Henry, D'Ambois and the
     ladies exeunt:

And hope you, madam, will take one carouse   [*To the Duchess.*
For reconcilement of your lord and servant.

> *Duchess.* If I should fail, my lord, some other lady
> Would be found there to do that for my servant.
> *Monsieur.* Any of these here?
> *Duchess.*   Nay, I know not that.
> *Bussy.*—Think your thoughts like my mistress, honour'd lady?
> *Tamyra.* I think not on you, sir; y'are one I know not.
> *Bussy.* Cry you mercy, madam!
> *Montsurry.*   Oh, sir, has she met you?

132   A, proper; B, worthy.

141   A, gadding; B, ranging.

144   A, and indeed; B, for you know.

152–3   A, being old/And cunning in his choice of lairs and haunts; B, the hart/Being old and cunning in his lairs and haunts.

155–6   A, yet where his custom is/ To beat his vault, and he ruts with his hind; B, yet where, behind some queach,/ He breaks his gall, and rutteth with his hind.

160   A, greatest women; B, chiefest women.

164   A, an excellent; B, the cunningest.

166–70   B emends:

> *Monsieur.* I have broken
> The ice to it already with the woman
> Of your chaste lady, and conceive good hope
> I shall wade thorough to some wished shore
> At our next meeting.
> *Montsurry.* Nay, there's small hope there.
> *Guise.* Take say of her, my lord, she comes most fitly.
>
>   *Enter* Charlotte, Annable, Pero.
>
> *Mons.* Starting back?
> *Guise.* Y'are engaged, indeed.

178   A, concerning; B, of.

179   A, promised; B, sworn to thee.

180   A, on that you have sworn; B, on that assurance.

184–5 A, so it be not to one that will betray thee; B, so we reach our objects.

189   A, into earth; B, to perdition.

191   A, wondering; B, watching. A, stole; B, stole up.

194   A, and she set close at a banquet; B, and herself reading a letter.

198   A, No, my lord; B, I swear.

199–201 A omits 'Why . . . Oh, the'.

205   After 'her woman', B adds, 'never dreaming of D'Ambois'.

207   A, his; B, this.

208–9 A, could; B, should. A, performed; B, made.

216–20 B omits the speeches of Charlotte and Guise.

224–225 A, your Lady, or the countess Beaupré; B, your Lady or the Lady Beaupré.

227   B omits 'if she marks it'.

228 A, put off all; B, disguise all.
231 A, at; B, from.
238 A, We be; B, We are.
251 A, if; B, when.
256 A, your portion; B, your great portion.
261–2 A, end of you; B, end of it.
266 A, I leave; B, we leave.
267 A, my mercy; B, our mercies.
274 A, is negligent; B, is thought negligent.
281 A, horrible; B, miraculous.
286 A, my lord, 'tis true and more; B, Well, my lord, more.
287 After 'banquet' B adds: *Guise*. Come, my lord; I have the
　　　blind side of one of them.
292 A, monster-formed clouds; B, dark and standing fogs.
297–304 B omits 'I will conceal. . . . no limit', and substitutes:

　　　But what a cloud of sulphur have I drawn
　　　Up to my bosom in this dangerous secret!
　　　Which if my haste with any spark should light
　　　Ere D'Ambois were engag'd in some sure plot,
　　　I were blown up; he would be, sure, my death.
　　　Would I had never known it, for before
　　　I shall persuade th' importance to Montsurry,
　　　And make him with some studied stratagem
　　　Train D'Ambois to his wreak, his maid may tell it;
　　　Or I (out of my fiery thirst to play
　　　With the fell tiger, up in darkness tied,
　　　And give it some light) make it quite break loose.
　　　I fear it afore heaven, and will not see
　　　D'Ambois again, till I have told Montsurry,
　　　And set a snare with him to free my fears.
　　　Who's there?
　　　　　　　　　Enter MAFFÉ.

　　　Maffé.　　My lord?
　　　Monsieur.　　　　　Go call the Count Montsurry,
　　　And make the doors fast; I will speak with none
　　　Till he come to me.
　　　Maffé.　　　　Well, my lord.　　　　　　[*Exiturus.*
　　　Monsieur.　　　　　　Or else
　　　Send you some other, and see all the doors
　　　Made safe yourself, I pray; haste, fly about it.
　　　　Maffé. You'll speak with none but with the Count Montsurry?
　　　　Monsieur. With none but he, except it be the Guise.
　　　　Maffé. See, even by this there's one exception more;
　　　Your Grace must be more firm in the command,
　　　Or else shall I as weakly execute.
　　　The Guise shall speak with you?
　　　　Monsieur.　　　　　He shall, I say.
　　　　Maffé. And Count Montsurry?
　　　　Monsieur.　　　　　Ay, and Count Montsurry.
　　　　Maffé. Your Grace must pardon me, that I am bold

To urge the clear and full sense of your pleasure;
Which whensoever I have known, I hope
Your Grace will say I hit it to a hair.
    Monsieur. You have.
    Maffé.   I hope so, or I would be glad—
    Monsieur. I pray thee get thee gone; thou art so tedious
In the strict form of all thy services,
That I had better have one negligent.
You hit my pleasure well, when D'Ambois hit you;
Did you not, think you?
    Maffé.   D'Ambois? Why, my lord—
    Monsieur. I pray thee talk no more, but shut the doors:
Do what I charge thee.
    Maffé.   I will, my lord, and yet
I would be glad the wrong I had of D'Ambois—
    Monsieur. Precious, then it is a fate that plagues me
In this man's foolery! I may be murther'd
While he stands on protection of his folly.
Avaunt about thy charge!
    Maffé.   I go, my lord.
—I had my head broke in his faithful service;
I had no suit the more, nor any thanks,
And yet my teeth must still be hit with D'Ambois—
D'Ambois, my lord, shall know—
    Monsieur.   The devil and D'Ambois!
                                  [Exit MAFFÉ.

How am I tortur'd with this trusty fool!
Never was any curious in his place
To do things justly, but he was an ass;
We cannot find one trusty that is witty,
And therefore bear their disproportion.
Grant, thou great star and angel of my life,
A sure lease of it but for some few days,
That I may clear my bosom of the snake
I cherish'd there, and I will then defy
All check to it but Nature's, and her altars
Shall crack with vessels crown'd with every liquor
Drawn from her highest and most bloody humours.
I fear him strangely, his advanced valour
Is like a spirit rais'd without a circle,
Endangering him that ignorantly rais'd him,
And for whose fury he hath learnt no limit.

Enter MAFFÉ *hastily.*

    Maffé. I cannot help it: what should I do more?
As I was gathering a fit guard to make
My passage to the doors, and the doors sure,
The man of blood is enter'd.
    Monsieur.   Rage of death!
If I had told the secret, and he knew it,
Thus had I been endanger'd.
                              [Enter D'AMBOIS.
               My sweetheart!

307 A, head; B, brows.

310   A, Sir; B, Prince.
312-17   Wilt thou not leave . . . all things. B substitutes:

> *Monsieur.* Wilt thou not leave that wrongful supposition?
> *Bussy.* Why wrongful to suppose the doubtless right
> To the succession worth the thinking?
> *Monsieur.* Well, leave these jests! How I am overjoy'd
> With thy wish'd presence, and how fit thou com'st,
> For, of mine honour, I was sending for thee.
> *Bussy.* To what end?
> *Monsieur.*   Only for thy company,
> Which I have still in thought; but that's no payment
> On thy part made with personal appearance.
> Thy absence so long suffer'd often times
> Put me in some little doubt thou dost not love me.
> Wilt thou do one thing therefore now sincerely?
> *Bussy.* Ay, anything, but killing of the King.
> *Monsieur.* Still in that discord, and ill-taken note?
> How most unseasonable thou playest the cuckoo,
> In this thy fall of friendship!
> *Bussy.*   Then do not doubt
> That there is any act within my nerves,
> But killing of the King, that is not yours.

318   A, and now by all my love; B, to prove which by my love.
320   A, that affection; B, that still-flourishing tree,/ With what-
      soever may hereafter spring,
324   After what I think of you? B inserts: *Monsieur.* Plain as
      truth.
337   A, begin, and speak me simply. B, pay me home; I'll bide it
      bravely.
346   A, wife; B, strumpet.
360   A, I carry; B, hath reference.
386   A, y'are; B, you are.
398   A, A perfect; B, The purest.

      Act IV, Scene i
  5   A, fare; B, foul.
 12   A, light; B, height.
 16   A, images; B, idols.
 20   After 'sad', B adds a further line: 'So then they rule in men,
      not men in them.'
 23   A, motions; B, faculty.
25-8   In B, Montsurry speaks these lines.
 27   A, predominance; B, divided empires.
 28   A, claim; B, prove.
 37   A, Of tyrannous law; B, of privilege, law.
 52   A, bound; B, bar.
 64   A, but; B, and.

67   A, it strike; B, it not strike.

68–72 A 'No, I think . . . and slit'. B emends:

> *Bussy.* If he be wise, not.
> *Monsieur.* What? Not if I should name the gardener
> That I would have him think hath grafted him?
> *Bussy.* So the large licence that your greatness uses
> To jest at all men, may be taught indeed
> To make a difference of the grounds you play on,
> Both in the men you scandal, and the matter.
> *Monsieur.* As how? As how?
> *Bussy.*   Perhaps led with a train,
> Where you may have your nose made less and slit,

86   A, toughness; B, roughness.

90   A, into air; B, into the air.

97   A, spirit; B, mind.

98   A, effect; B, desert.

106 A, is coming to afflict; B, steals on to ravish.

145–6 A, Sweet lord, clear up those eyes, for shame of noblesse;
      Merciless creature! But it is enough; B emends:

> Sweet lord, clear up those eyes, for shame of noblesse,
> Unbend that masking forehead; whence is it
> You rush upon her with these Irish wars,
> More full of sound than hurt? But it is enough,

165 A, loathed; B, just.

172 A, hand; B, fingers.

185 A, Even to his teeth whence, in mine honour's soil; B, Even
     to his venomed teeth, from whose cursed seed.

197–9 B emends:

> To see the dangerous paper; papers hold
> Oft-times the forms and copies of our souls,
> And, though the world despise them, are the prizes
> Of all our honours; make your honour then
> A hostage for it, and with it confer

202 A, much; B, well.

207 A, my lord; B, this touch.

222 A, I'll attend your lordship; B, But I will to him.

224 A, speak; B, meet.

225 B adds another line: To him, my lord, and I'll to cursing
     him.

Act IV, Scene ii

B begins the scene with the entry of D'Ambois and the
Friar, and eighteen lines of dialogue, after which Tamyra
enters:

Enter D'AMBOIS *and* FRIAR.

Bussy. I am suspicious, my most honour'd father,
By some of Monsieur's cunning passages,
That his still ranging and contentious nostrils,
To scent the haunts of Mischief have so us'd
The vicious virtue of his busy sense,
That he trails hotly of him, and will rouse him,
Driving him all enrag'd and foaming on us;
And therefore have entreated your deep skill
In the command of good aërial spirits,
To assume these magic rites, and call up one
To know if any have reveal'd unto him
Anything touching my dear love and me.
    Friar. Good son, you have amaz'd me but to make
The least doubt of it, it concerns so nearly
The faith and reverence of my name and order.
Yet will I justify, upon my soul,
All I have done; if any spirit i' th' earth or air
Can give you the resolve, do not despair.

3   A, eyes; B, cursed eyes.
6   B omits entry of Bussy and Friar.
7   B omits 'Father'.
9–10 After 'infamy', B, emends:

                    Our love is known;
Your Monsieur hath a paper where is writ
Some secret tokens that decipher it.
    Bus. What cold dull Northern brain, what fool but he
Durst take . . .

30   A, ye; B, you.
79   A and B give the Friar's speech to Monsieur.
89   A, wherein you; B, where you may.
101 A, stuff; B, lines.
116 A, ill; B, cruelly.
119 A, I hope it be, at least, if not a volume; B, I hope it rather
     be a bitter volume.
120 After 'perjury', B adds: *Guise.* To you, my lord. *Monsieur.*
     To me? Now . . .'
130 stain. A, stay; B, die.
131 A, with; B, In.
137 A, And let him curb his rage with policy; B, And curb his
     valour with your policies.
168 A, print; B, taint.
172 A, from; B, by.

Act V, Scene i
B adds four lines to open the scene:

    Tamyra. Oh, help me, father!
    Friar.   Impious earl, forbear.

Take violent hand from her, or, by mine order,
The King shall force thee.
    Montsurry.   'Tis not violent;
Come you not willingly?
    Tamyra.   Yes, good my lord.

17   A, than it; B, than that.
24   A, hateful; B, secret.
28   A, touch; B, tread.
31   A, cease; B, cease your terrors.
36   A, God; B, Heaven. A, ye; B, you.
38   A, heart; B, breast.
39   A, Ope the seven times-heat; B, Stand the opening.
41   A, O; B, For. A, cares; B, woes.
44   A, enraged; B, devouring.
53   A, God; B, Heaven.
61   A, laden for thy lust; B, rigged with quench for lust!
84   A, distract; B, devour. A, state; B, consort.
88   A, sins; B, faults.
122   A, In doing their justice there; thine arms have lost; B, In
             doing their justice there with any show/ Of the like
             cruelty; thine arms have lost.
132   A, still; B, ever.
133   A, like in ill; B, parallel.
166   A, innocent; B, worthy.
168   A, in; B, with.

Act V, Scene ii
This scene is placed at V, iii in B.
8   A, cracks; B, nods.
9   A, my; B, dear.
14   After 'my love', B adds: And now his restless spirit would
            forewarn me / Of some plot dangerous and imminent.
15   A, utmost; B, upper.
47   A, see; B, shine.
48   A, sense is; B, men are.
74   A, and force; B, or force. A, soul; B, life.
83–8   'Hail . . . presence'. B emends:

    Montsurry. Hail to my worthy son.
    Bussy.   Oh, lying Spirit,
To say the Friar was dead! I'll now believe
Nothing of all his forg'd predictions.
My kind and honour'd father, well reviv'd!
I have been frighted with your death and mine,
And told my mistress' hand should be my death,
If I obey'd this summons.
    Montsurry.   I believ'd
Your love had been much clearer than to give

Any such doubt a thought, for she is clear,
And having freed her husband's jealousy
(Of which her much abus'd hand here is witness)
She prays, for urgent cause, your instant presence.
  Bussy. Why, then your Prince of Spirits may be call'd
The Prince of liars.
  Montsurry.   Holy Writ so calls him.

Act V, Scene iii

1-56 In B these lines form V. ii, together with the following new
      lines after 'all men's hate'.

> *Enter* MONTSURRY *disguised [as the* FRIAR] *with the* MURTHERERS.

Away, my lord; you are perfectly disguis'd,
Leave us to lodge your ambush.
  Montsurry.   Speed me, vengeance!   [*Exit.*
  Monsieur. Resolve, my masters, you shall meet with one
Will try what proofs your privy coats are made on:
When he is enter'd, and you hear us stamp,
Approach, and make all sure.
  Murtherers.   We will, my lord.   [*Exeunt.*

 3   A, who; B, that.
 7-11 Omitted in B.
12   A, It falls out they incur; B, Not knowing what they say,
13   A, mass; B, deal.
18   A, we call; B, she calls.
19   A, believe should; B, belief must.
21   A, Right as; B, Even as.
22   A, men think; B, methinks. A, guard them; B, guard.
30   A, decorum; B, proportion.
33   A, an absolute; B, a perfect.
34   A, whole; B, full.
37   A, Why, you shall; B, Yet shall you.
45   A, rages; B, rage. A, th' root; B, the root.
46   A, So this full creature now shall reel and fall; B, So this
     whole man,/ That will not wind with every crooked
     way / Trod by the servile world, shall reel and fall.
47   A, purblind; B, blind-born.
51   A, Euxine; B, Euxian.
57-60 A, Revive . . . devise; B emends:

> *Ghost.* Up with these stupid thoughts, still loved daughter,
> And strike away this heartless trance of anguish.
> Be like the sun, and labour in eclipses;
> Look to the end of woes: oh, can you sit
> Mustering the horrors of your servant's slaughter
> Before your contemplation, and not study

63   A, engaged; B, revenged.
69   A, 'Tis the just curse of our abused creation; B, It is the
     misery of our creation.

70–4 B omits and substitutes:

> Your true friend,
> Led by your husband, shadow'd in my weed,
> Now enters the dark vault.
>   *Tamyra.*   But, my dearest father,
> Why will not you appear to him yourself,
> And see that none of these deceits annoy him?
>   *Ghost.* My power is limited; alas! I cannot.
> All that I can do—See, the cave opens!   [*Exit.*

75 After 'murthered'; B has s.d. *Enter Monsieur and Guise above.*

84 After 'pierceth', B adds:

> If I scape Monsieur's 'pothecary shops,
> Foutre for Guise's shambles! 'Twas ill plotted;
> They should have maul'd me here,
> When I was rising. I am up and ready.

88–9 A, my fate./ Dare they not come?; B, my fate. *Monsieur, Guise.* Why enter not the coward villains? *Bussy.* Dare they not come?

137–140 These lines are not in A.

166 A, And; B, Now.

182 A, 'gainst; B, in.

183 A, endless; B, drifts of.

196–8 Omitted in B.

206 A, sitting; B, kneeling.

217–8 Omitted in B.

230 After 'conscience', B adds: *Monsieur.* Come, let's away; my senses are not proof / Against those plaints. *Exeunt Guise and Monsieur. D'Ambois is borne off.*

265–7 Omitted in B.

268–74 In B, these lines are placed at line 193, after the death of Bussy.

270 A, Join flames with Hercules; B, Jove flames with her rules.

272 cracked. A and B, crack.

Printed in Great Britain by Fletcher & Son Ltd, Norwich